What they're saying about N

Michael Suchman and Ethan Ciment are my plant-based supermen. These two gay, vegan Brooklynites are teaching the world that the coolest thing to be is compassionate. And they are proving that peaceful food is not just seditious and nutritious, but also delicious!

—Jane Velez-Mitchell, TV journalist, *New York Times* best-selling author, and founder of JaneUnChained

The diverse, eclectic flavors of New York City are reflected in *NYC Vegan*, only bigger, better, and with more chutzpah. Ethan and Michael have their finger on the pulse of the various tastes that make up the Big Apple's quintessential edibles, and they have the talent and passion for recipe- and community-building that will make this your go-to vegan cookbook. What else would you expect from two adorable mensches from Brooklyn?

—Jasmin Singer, author of *Always Too Much and Never Enough* and senior editor at *Veg-News Magazine*

Fun, creative, veganized classic recipes from the heart. Michael and Ethan share their vegan passion for New York and its bursts of international flavor. Their recipes take you on a vegan gastronomical tour of the Big Apple. We love to feed them at Candle 79 and the Candle Cafes, in our mutual effort to raise the vegan bar and make it delicious!

—Joy Pierson and Bart Potenza, authors and founders of Candle Cafe, Candle 79, and Candle Cafe West

There's no food like New York City food, and Suchman and Ciment capture flawlessly the flavors, diversity, and inimitable personality of the Great Big Apple in recipes that also reflect one of the city's newer charms, being a worldwide center of vegan culture and cuisine. Not only that, but these sophisticated recipes are accessible and reproducible, even in a tiny New York City kitchen.

—Victoria Moran, author of *Main Street Vegan*

New York City is America's kitchen and New Yorkers Michael Suchman and Ethan Ciment's new book, *NYC Vegan*, is a fantastic taste of the Big Apple. It's filled with an amazing assortment of recipes for celebrated dishes, from uptown to downtown, East Side to West Side, and from every ethnic group. You'll want to try them all. The book is a wonderful guidebook, as well. You don't have to be vegan or from New York to love this book. I happen to be a NYC vegan myself and have waited a long time for just this book.

— Fran Costigan, author *Vegan Chocolate*; director of Vegan Baking and Pastry, Rouxbe Cooking School

New York City is famous for its glamour, fashion, art, cultural diversity and of course its food! This book not only celebrates what makes New York City great but elevates traditional favorites to a compassionate place in a delicious way that everyone will love.

—Annie Shannon, co-author of *Betty Goes Vegan*

NYC Vegan is a terrifically tasty tribute to the diversity of the Big Apple's culinary past, present, and future. Michael and Ethan are the perfect virtual tour guides, dropping heaps of foodie factoids while you wind through their ethnically rich collection of well-crafted, veganized classics.

—Brian L. Patton, vegan chef and cookbook author

NYC Vegan is a creative tribute to the cuisines and dishes that make up New York City's rich culinary heritage. It's more than that, though: this book is proof that it is possible to eat a compassionate diet while remaining connected to culture and tradition. Warm, welcoming, and beautifully photographed, the book is a must-have for plant-based eaters and for anyone who loves diverse, vibrant, global food.

—Gena Hamshaw, author of *Food52 Vegan*

NYC Vegan is not just the definitive guide to recreating the foods of the city that never sleeps. It's also part history lesson, part travel guide (complete with restaurant recommendations) and part insiders glimpse into what real New Yorkers eat. The foods of New York really are the foods of the world, and here we have it all, veganized for us, inviting us to the table, the lunch counter, the farmers market, the street cart, the subway platform, uptown or downtown, or any one of the city's boroughs. Let's eat New York!

—Michelle Schwegmann, co-founder of the Herbivore Clothing Company and author of *Eat Like You Give a Damn*

NYC
Vegan

Iconic Recipes for a Taste of the Big Apple

MICHAEL SUCHMAN & ETHAN CIMENT
THE VEGAN MOS

Foreword by Alan Cumming

VEGAN HERITAGE PRESS, LLC
Woodstock • Virginia

NYC Vegan: Iconic Recipes for a Taste of the Big Apple (Copyright © 2017 by Michael Suchman and Ethan Ciment)

ISBN: 978-1-941252-33-8
First Edition, May 2017
10 9 8 7 6 5 4 3 2 1

Vegan Heritage Press, LLC books are available at quantity discounts. For ordering information, please visit our website at www.veganheritagepress.com or write the publisher at Vegan Heritage Press, LLC, P.O. Box 628, Woodstock, VA 22664-0628.

Library of Congress Cataloging-in-Publication Data

Names: Suchman, Michael, 1971- author. | Ciment, Ethan, 1971- author.
Title: NYC vegan : iconic recipes for a taste of the Big Apple / Michael Suchman and Ethan Ciment.
Description: First editon. | Woodstock, Virginia : Vegan Heritage Press, [2017] | Includes index.
Identifiers: LCCN 2016048251 (print) | LCCN 2016051300 (ebook) | ISBN 9781941252338 (pbk.) | ISBN 9781941252345 (epub) | ISBN 9781941252352 (prc)
Subjects: LCSH: Vegan cooking--New York (State)--New York. | LCGFT: Cookbooks.
Classification: LCC TX771 .S827 2017 (print) | LCC TX771 (ebook) | DDC 641.5/63609747--dc23
LC record available at https://lccn.loc.gov/2016048251

Photo credits: Cover and interior food photos by Jackie Sobon. New York City scenes from stock photo sources. Back Cover Photos (left to right): New York-Style Bagels, page 40; Manhattan Glam Chowder, page 53; Classic NYC Pizza, page 96; and New York Cheesecake, page 161.

Disclaimer: The information provided in this book should not be taken as medical advice. If you require a medical diagnosis or prescription, or if you are contemplating any major dietary change consult a qualified health-care provider. Neither the publisher nor the author are responsible for readers' health issues.

Publisher's Note: The information in this book is correct and complete to the best of our knowledge. The publisher is not responsible for specific health or allergy issues regarding ingredients used in this book.

Vegan Heritage Press, LLC books are distributed by Andrews McMeel Publishing.

Printed in the United States of America

Dedication

To our beloved Chandler, who started us on our journey into veganism.

Each day with you was a gift. You taught us to appreciate the good days and stay grounded in the present moment. You live on in our hearts and we know you continue to watch over us from the Rainbow Bridge.

We will always love you.

Daddy and Dad-E

Contents

FOUR: POWER LUNCH

FIVE: START SPREADING THE NEWS

SIX: SUPPER CLUB

SEVEN: FARMERS' MARKET

EIGHT: ON THE SIDE

NINE: HOW SWEET IT IS

TEN: BEING VEGAN IN NEW YORK CITY

Foreword

I don't think I can truly say I have ever enjoyed reading a cookbook before.

Sure, I have been entertained, occasionally illuminated, and most often relieved to have found something I could whip up at the last minute with the ingredients I had available. But enjoy? As in actually wanting to go back and read bits of the book again?! Nah.

But this book is the exception. Michael Suchman and Ethan Ciment have managed to do something very special: express their love for and allegiance to New York City, then reinterpret that city's classic dishes for a new and different generation. And in so doing, they define and reinvigorate what makes New York City so great. It's why I love it, too.

For what is New York if not a city that is constantly changing? When I hear people start to moan about how it used to be so much better in the old days and how the city has changed, I want to slap them and say, "Of course it's changed! Change is why we're here! New York City is always changing, it's always moving, it's always redefining itself—and that's what makes it so exciting!"

Mourning the loss of a favorite restaurant or bar or building is one thing, but not realizing the potential for something new and exciting in that loss means that maybe those people and New York City aren't as good a match as they once were.

This book is the essence of New York. It pays homage to the great dishes and cuisines that have been a part of the city's landscape for so long, then shows you how to veganize them and enjoy them in a whole new way. It simultaneously celebrates the past and reinvents the present. This is the literary cookbook equivalent of Madonna, people!!!

If you're a baby vegan or an old ham like me (or even just vegan-curious), this book is all you will ever need to have a successful vegan life. Seriously. It tells you how to make not just your favorite dishes, but the basic components of them. And its tone and wit will demystify and un-crunchify even the most clichéd stereotypes about the vegan lifestyle.

This book is the quintessence of New York, and I love—and am happy to be in—both!

Alan Cumming
actor, author, activist

Introduction

New York City. Whether you call it New York, the City, the Big Apple, NYC, or Gotham, everyone knows what city you are talking about. New York City is truly the capital of the world. The bright lights and constant energy of this city attract people from all over the globe. More than one-third of the people who live here were born in another country. Over eight hundred different languages are spoken here. This unique multicultural mix of people is what gives New York City its edge and is what gives all of us who live here a higher sense of ambition and energy. We New Yorkers respect and embrace our differences and our diversity.

The idea for doing a cookbook came out of a dinner party we held in our apartment. A number of friends at the party were published vegan cookbook authors and strongly encouraged us to consider writing one of our own. When the party was over, we would occasionally bounce ideas off one another, but nothing really felt right. We were stuck on the theme of the book—each idea we had did not fit with who we are. So we decided that if we were going to write a cookbook, we needed a theme that had a personal connection to us. One day, Ethan suddenly said, "We're New Yorkers. We love New York City. We should do a book on New York City food," and that was all it took. We are New Yorkers—Michael was born here and Ethan moved here over twenty-six years ago. New York City is where we met, dated, got married, and built our lives together. Because this city has played such a critically important role in our lives, we want to celebrate it, and this book is our love letter to our hometown.

In *NYC Vegan*, we pay homage to the diversity of America's largest city as represented in the cuisines that immigrants to this city brought with them. Of course, with a city as large and diverse as New York, it's impossible to represent every ethnicity and cultural background in one book. Therefore, we will focus on showcasing many of the classic foods that people associate with New York City. From blintzes and churros to Italian ices and knishes, we will share our recipes for vegan versions of the foods that New York made famous. We will also take you along on a journey through the different neighborhoods of the city, such as the center of Greek American life in Astoria, where you can enjoy a traditional tzatziki. We can hop on the G train to eat savory Polish pierogi in Greenpoint, and then take a taxi up to Arthur Avenue in the Bronx for a bowl of minestrone. Whether it's matzoh brei on the Lower East Side or caramel corn at Yankee Stadium, we will show you how to make delectable vegan versions of your favorite New York City foods.

The vegan community in New York City is like no other in the world. In a city of over 8 million people, this vegan community feels more like a closely knit village. Vegans in New York City defy the stereotype of the aloof New Yorker who never makes eye contact with or speaks to their neighbor. Whether we meet at a pop-up market or a veg fest, a fundraiser or a local farm sanctuary, the crowd is always filled with people who know you or who want to know you. We learned this firsthand in September 2013 after starting our blog, VeganMos.com. At that time, we started to attend more local vegan events and were stunned by how warmly we were embraced by total strangers. These folks supported and encouraged us since day one and made us feel a level of connection and community we never expected to find in such a large and all-too-often lonely city.

New York City gives us hope. It is akin to a giant tossed salad: many different ingredients coming together to create something delicious and colorful, each ingredient keeping its own identity but complementing and blending well with the others. The result of this combination is something greater and more beautiful than the sum of its parts. If we can peacefully coexist and celebrate the diversity of humanity in such a geographically small and densely populated area as New York City, surely we can extend this to the rest of our country, to the world, and to the trillions of nonhuman animals with whom we share the Earth, our only home.

One
THE FLAVORS OF NEW YORK CITY

Certain foods conjure up images of New York City: a slice of pizza, an egg cream soda, and, of course, bagels. There are also many foods that were created in the City and went on to become so well known that their New York roots were forgotten, such as eggs Benedict, General Tso's chicken, a Reuben sandwich, and Waldorf salad. Thanks to New York's wide ethnic diversity and the largest subway system in the world, we can eat Indian dal, Polish pierogi, Columbian arepas, and Israeli falafel in a single day without ever leaving the City.

With so much delicious food to choose from, we felt it was time for vegans everywhere to be able to get a taste of the Big Apple. This book draws inspiration from the various cultures that make up the City as well as our own personal experiences of living in New York. Whether it's Greek Avgolemeno Soup in Astoria or our New-Fashioned Jewish Chick'n Soup from the Lower East Side, there are simple ways to make this city's food vegan. If you're looking for an Italian lasagna like they serve in Staten Island, loaded with fresh homemade ricotta, or you are craving a classic Puerto Rican mofongo like they serve in Spanish Harlem, we will teach you how to bring the flavors of New York City into your kitchen.

When you say "New York," most people automatically think of Manhattan. This conjures up images of Central Park, Wall Street, the Empire State Building, Times Square, and the Freedom Tower. The reality of New York City is that Manhattan is just one of the five boroughs, and only the third most populated. More than three out of four New Yorkers live in the outer boroughs: the Bronx, Brooklyn, Queens, or Staten Island. New York, America's largest city, is home to 8.5 million people living in just 303 square miles. That is the entire populations of Montana, Kansas, New Mexico, Rhode Island, and Hawaii compressed into an area smaller than half the size of the island of Maui.

Some of the largest ethnic populations outside of their countries of origin exist in New York City. The metropolitan area is home to the largest Jewish community outside Israel. New York City is also home to nearly a quarter of the United States' Indian Americans and boasts the largest Indian population in the Western Hemisphere. The largest African American community of any city in America is found in New York City. The City is home to more than one million Asian Americans, a number greater than the Asian American populations of San Francisco and Los Angeles combined. In fact, New York City has six Chinatowns! The Puerto Rican population of New York City is the largest outside of Puerto Rico. Thanks to the large number of Italians that immigrated to the city in the early twentieth century, there are several Little Italy neighborhoods throughout the five boroughs. These examples are not meant to exclude other ethnic groups such as the Irish, Dominicans, Pakistanis, Russians, or Germans who each have a very large and well-represented presence in New York City.

To achieve this population density, New York City builds upward. Our homes are mostly apartments, stacked atop one another like books on shelves. Kitchens in New York City apartments tend to be much smaller than in other parts of the country, but with over twenty-four thousand restaurants, most New Yorkers don't mind. In fact, it is not uncommon for New Yorkers to use their ovens and cupboards as additional storage space as square footage comes at a premium.

New York City is a food Mecca. New Yorkers and fans of New York City want to be able to enjoy classic New York City foods. Our goal with this cookbook is to enable vegans and nonvegans alike to enjoy vegan versions of timeless and iconic New York City cuisine. The recipes we selected for *NYC Vegan* showcase the diverse flavors of New York City and its classic foods. As self-trained cooks, we understand that cooking can and should be simple, so our recipes don't require any special ingredients. We want everybody, regardless of skill level, to be able to make every recipe in the book. To us, cooking delicious food is an expression of love and a desire to share that with others. Throughout this book, we will share personal stories of what the recipes mean to us, how they relate to New York City, as well as share fun facts about this amazing city we call home.

We consider ourselves to be home cooks. We learned from watching our mothers and grandmothers, television programs, and from reading cookbooks. There was a lot of trial and error in developing our cooking style and skills. We both feel that cooking should be fun and that approaching the kitchen is something we all can do, but we have to keep a light and positive attitude about it. Many people get themselves worked up before they go into the kitchen. They start to tense up, freak out, and they're nearly a basket case before even starting to preheat the oven. What's the worst thing that can happen when you try new recipes? The recipe might not turn out like you wanted, and you'll have to order takeout instead. There's no reason to take something as natural and inherently human as preparing food for yourself and your family and make it into a mystical science that requires advanced training. Everybody can and should be able to cook.

Ethan was vegan for almost two years before Michael. During that time, Michael worked from home and did the bulk of the cooking. He had to figure out ways to cook for both an omnivore and a vegan without having to make two completely different meals. This often meant having grains, veggies, and other sides that were vegan and then having a vegan and nonvegan main. Eventually, the challenge enticed him, and Michael began trying to figure out how to make vegan versions of the nonvegan foods he had been making. This was a hit-and-miss process; sometimes things worked right off the bat, and other times, well, not so much. Michael learned how to use seitan, tofu, and tempeh in place of animal meats. However, when it came to baking, the learning took a little more time. Knowing what to use in place of eggs presented its own set of challenges. Once we learned to identify the reason for the eggs in a recipe (leavening or binding) we could better determine an ideal substitution. That means that even though our recipes may call for seitan, you can still use tofu, tempeh, or even Soy Curls. If we call for Ener-G Egg Replacer, but you prefer to use Follow Your Heart brand's VeganEgg, do it! We just want you to have fun in the kitchen exploring new foods and recipes and finding what works for you. As home cooks, we know that there is not one "right" way to cook.

One last note before we get to the recipes: occasionally a recipe will be preceded by either "Michael" or "Ethan." This is simply our way of letting you know there is something personal to one of us about a particular recipe. So, with that said, let's cook!

Two
THE BASICS

All the recipes in this section are commercially available, but it's great to be able to make these items for yourself. Not only do homemade foods taste better, but you're in control of the ingredients so you can adjust them to your own preferences. Treat this section like a visit to the City—sure, you can get around quickly by subway, but because you are underground you miss seeing the city itself. Sometimes, you want to take a taxi or simply walk to truly see everything the City has to offer. Similarly, making your own basics gives you a new appreciation for the store-bought versions. The recipes in this chapter will be used throughout the rest of the book, and while we encourage you to make them and use them, we promise not to tell on you if you buy the commercial equivalents. Your secret will be safe with us.

Sure, you can buy any type of nut milk, but making your own allows you to play with the flavors. Named to honor the classic New York City coffee that has been around since 1932, this recipe is Ethan's go-to homemade vegan milk that he especially loves to have in a strong cup of dark coffee. Though you can use cheesecloth to strain your milk, we prefer to use a reusable nylon nut-milk bag. These are inexpensive and widely available.

CHOCK FULL O' NUTS MILK

Makes 3 1/2 cups

1/2 cup raw Brazil nuts
1/4 cup raw almonds
1/3 cup raw cashews
4 cups filtered water, plus more for soaking
3 Medjool dates, pitted, or 1 tablespoon agave nectar
1/4 teaspoon salt
1 teaspoon vanilla extract, optional

1. In a large bowl, combine the Brazil nuts, almonds, and cashews. Cover with several inches of filtered water and soak for at least 8 hours, preferably overnight. Drain the nuts and rinse well.

2. In a high-speed blender, combine the soaked nuts, 4 cups filtered water, dates, salt, and vanilla (if using). Blend on high speed for 2 minutes, until thick and creamy.

3. Pour half the mixture into a nut-milk bag and allow it to drain over a large bowl. As the liquid volume decreases, gently squeeze and massage the bag to expel all liquid until you are left with a solid, dry paste. Discard the paste and repeat with the remaining half of the mixture.

4. Transfer the milk to a glass bottle or mason jar. It will keep in the refrigerator for 3 days.

In New York City, pizzerias are as common as nail salons and coffee shops. And while it's a treat to impulsively drop into a pizza joint and grab a slice of vegan pizza, it's always better when you can make exactly the type of pizza you want at home. This dough is not only used for making Classic NYC Pizza (page 96) but can also be used for Cinnamon Rolls (page 39) for breakfast or Zeppole (page 172) for dessert.

PIZZA DOUGH

Makes 2 pounds dough (for 2 large or 8 individual pizzas)

1 (1/4-ounce) package active dry yeast
1 1/2 teaspoons sugar
1 cup warm water (110°F to 115°F)
3 cups unbleached all-purpose flour
1 teaspoon salt
2 tablespoons extra-virgin olive oil, plus more for greasing the bowl

1. In a small bowl, dissolve the yeast and sugar in the warm water. Set aside to rest for 10 minutes.

2. In the bowl of a stand mixer, combine the flour and salt. Add the yeast mixture and oil to the bowl and mix well to make a soft dough. (If you don't have a stand mixer, you can do this with a wooden spoon.) Keep mixing until the dough comes away from the sides of the bowl and forms a ball. If the dough is too sticky, sprinkle with an additional 1 teaspoon flour and keep mixing.

3. If using a stand mixer, switch to the dough hook and knead the dough on low speed for 6 minutes. If kneading by hand, transfer the dough to a lightly floured surface and knead 5 to 10 minutes.

4. Lightly grease a large bowl with additional oil and put the dough in the bowl. Rotate it a few times to coat it lightly with oil. Cover the bowl with plastic wrap and let it rise 1 hour.

5. After 1 hour, uncover the dough and punch it down. Transfer the dough to a lightly floured work surface and knead for 1 minute. You can use the dough now, or let it rest for another hour. (It tastes better the longer you let it rest.) When ready to use the dough, cut the ball of dough in half. Use one half now and wrap one half in plastic wrap and freeze for another day.

This is our all-purpose seitan recipe. Its mild seasonings make it incredibly versatile. It works great in a wide array of recipes, including our Mofongo (page 93).

BASIC SEITAN

Makes 2 pounds

Seitan:
1 1/2 cups vital wheat gluten
1/4 cup nutritional yeast
2 tablespoons chickpea flour
1 teaspoon salt
3/4 cup vegetable broth
2 tablespoons soy sauce
2 tablespoons ketchup
2 tablespoons extra-virgin olive oil

Broth:
4 cups vegetable broth
4 cups water
1/2 cup soy sauce

1. Preheat the oven to 350°F. Line an 18 x 12-inch baking sheet with parchment paper and set aside.

2. In a large bowl, mix together the wheat gluten, nutritional yeast, chickpea flour, and salt. In a medium bowl, combine the vegetable broth, soy sauce, ketchup, and oil. Pour the broth mixture into the dry mixture and stir until the liquid is absorbed.

3. Use your hands and knead the mixture for 5 minutes. Divide the dough into 2 pieces and shape each into a loaf. Arrange the loaves on the prepared baking sheet and bake, uncovered, for 30 minutes.

4. When the seitan is almost done cooking, prepare the broth. Combine the vegetable broth, water, and soy sauce in a large pot, cover, and bring to a boil over high heat. Reduce the heat to just below a simmer.

5. Add the baked seitan to the broth and gently simmer for 1 hour. (Do not let it boil or you will develop air pockets in the seitan, resulting in a spongy texture.)

6. Remove the seitan from the broth and allow it to cool before using it in recipes. Store unused seitan in a covered container with some of the broth in the refrigerator for up to 2 weeks.

The combination of mushrooms, soy sauce, and red wine give this seitan a deep umami flavor. Use this Beefy Seitan in our Crispy Ginger Seitan (page 98) and Brisket of Seitan (page 100). It is also great when finely chopped or ground for our Street Meat Platter (page 65).

BEEFY SEITAN

Makes 3 pounds

Seitan:
8 ounces cremini mushrooms
1/4 cup soy sauce
1/4 cup red wine
2 cloves garlic
1 rounded teaspoon vegan beef bouillon paste or 1 vegan beef bouillon cube
1 1/4 cups vegetable broth
2 1/2 cups vital wheat gluten

Broth:
8 cups water
2 rounded teaspoons vegan beef bouillon paste or 2 vegan beef bouillon cubes

1. Preheat the oven to 350°F. Line an 18 x 12-inch baking sheet with parchment paper and set aside.

2. Combine the mushrooms, soy sauce, red wine, garlic, and bouillon paste in a food processor. Process until liquefied, about 2 minutes. Transfer the mixture to a large mixing bowl. Whisk the vegetable broth into the mushroom mixture. Using your hands, stir in the wheat gluten. Keep mixing with your hands to make a soft dough, about 5 minutes. If the dough seems too wet, add another 2 tablespoons wheat gluten.

3. Divide the dough in half and shape into 2 loaves. Place on the prepared baking sheet and bake for 30 minutes. While the dough is baking, prepare the simmering broth. In a large pot, combine the water and bouillon paste. Bring to a boil over high heat, then reduce to a low simmer.

4. When the seitan is done baking, add it to the broth and cover with the lid slightly ajar. Keep the broth at just below a simmer and do not allow it come to a boil or your seitan will get spongy. Simmer for 1 hour. After 1 hour, turn off the heat and allow the seitan to cool for a few hours in the broth. When cool enough to handle, remove the seitan and cool completely. Store unused seitan in a covered container with some of the broth in the refrigerator for up to 2 weeks.

This mild seitan makes use of poultry seasoning to suggest the flavor palette often associated with recipes that historically use chicken. This seitan is great for using in our Chick'n Pot Pie (page 88), Seitan Piccata (page 95), General Tso's Chick'n (page 102), and Southern-Fried Seitan (page 107). You can also use it in place of the Soy Curls in the Street Meat Platter (page 65).

CHICKEN-STYLE SEITAN

Makes about 1 1/2 pounds

1 1/2 cups cold water
1 rounded teaspoon vegan chicken bouillon paste or 1 vegan chicken bouillon cube
2 tablespoons extra-virgin olive oil
1 1/2 cups vital wheat gluten
1/4 cup chickpea flour
1/3 cup nutritional yeast
1 teaspoon garlic powder
1 1/2 teaspoons poultry seasoning
1/2 teaspoon paprika
1/2 teaspoon onion powder
1/2 teaspoon salt

1. In large measuring cup, whisk together the water, bouillon paste, and oil. Set aside.

2. In a large bowl, stir together the wheat gluten, chickpea flour, nutritional yeast, garlic powder, poultry seasoning, paprika, onion powder, and salt. Create a well in the center of the wheat gluten mixture and pour in the broth mixture. Use your hands to stir it together. Keep mixing with your hands to make a soft dough. Once you have a dough, keep kneading for 3 minutes to let the gluten develop. You can knead in the same bowl, or you can move the dough to a work surface. Let the dough rest for about 10 minutes, then knead for another 30 seconds. Cut the dough into 4 equal-size loaves.

3. While the dough is resting, set up a steamer for steaming. Tear off 4 (12-inch square) pieces of aluminum foil. Place a piece of dough in the center of each square of foil. Fold two sides of the foil over the dough, then fold over the other sides. You want the loaves to be completely covered, but with room to expand, so don't make the packages too tight.

4. Put the seitan packages into your steamer and steam for 30 minutes. If you need to stack them, be sure to switch them around after 15 minutes. Remove the seitan packages from the steamer and let them cool for at least 30 minutes before putting them in the fridge to chill for at least 1 hour to overnight. Store unused seitan in a covered container with some of the broth in the refrigerator for up to 2 weeks.

Soy Curls are the perfect gluten-free alternative to seitan. Try these in place of seitan in our Crispy Ginger Seitan (page 98).

BEEFY SOY CURLS

Makes 6 cups

1 rounded teaspoon vegan beef bouillon paste or 1 vegan beef bouillon cube
1/4 teaspoon garlic powder
3 cups hot water
1 (8-ounce) package Soy Curls

1. In a large bowl, dissolve the bouillon paste and garlic powder in the hot water. Add the Soy Curls and set aside for 10 minutes.

2. After 10 minutes, drain the Soy Curls and squeeze out as much water as possible. They are now ready to use in any recipe.

Did You Know?

The first underground line of the New York City subway system opened in October 1904, making it one of the world's oldest public rapid transit systems. Today, the subway has more stations than any other rapid transit system in the world: 469 at current count (but when the long awaited 2nd Avenue line opens, that number will increase). With over 233 miles of tracks, it is the fourth longest subway system in the world. When the subway first opened, the 150,000 riders that day only had to pay five cents for a trip. Today, the fare is $2.75 for a one-way ride, with over 5.7 million daily rides given. Stations are located throughout the Bronx, Brooklyn, Manhattan, and Queens, and all lines of the system (except the G train) pass through Manhattan, making it a convenient way to get around the City—unless you want to go to Staten Island, which has no direct connection to the New York City subway system. If you want to know how to get to Staten Island, read the sidebar on page 16.

We love to use these Soy Curls in our Street Meat Platter (page 65). We often use them in place of seitan in our General Tso's Chick'n (page 102) to make the dish gluten-free.

CHICKEN-STYLE SOY CURLS

Makes 6 cups

1 rounded teaspoon vegan chicken bouillon paste or 1 vegan chicken bouillon cube
1/4 teaspoon garlic powder
1/4 teaspoon onion powder
1/2 teaspoon paprika
3 cups hot water
1 (8-ounce) package Soy Curls

1. In a large bowl, dissolve the bouillon paste, garlic powder, onion powder, and paprika in the hot water. Add the Soy Curls and set aside for 10 minutes.

2. After 10 minutes, drain the Soy Curls and squeeze out as much water as possible. They are now ready to use in any recipe.

"Practically everybody in New York has half a mind to write a book—and does."

— Groucho Marx

Glass jars of grated Parmesan are fixtures in pizza joints and Italian restaurants all over New York City, where sprinkling it on your pizza or pasta is expected. Our four-ingredient version is great on Classic NYC Pizza (page 96), in Lasagna (page 86), on Roasted Asparagus (page 114), or anywhere else you would want a sprinkle of cheese.

CASHEW PARMESAN

Makes 1 cup

1 cup raw cashews
2 tablespoons nutritional yeast
1 teaspoon salt
1/4 teaspoon garlic powder

1. In a food processor, combine the cashews, nutritional yeast, salt, and garlic powder. Pulse until the ingredients form a fine meal resembling the consistency of grated Parmesan cheese.

2. Store the cashew Parmesan for up to 3 weeks in a covered container in the refrigerator.

Tourist Tip

The best free thing you can do in New York City is ride the Staten Island Ferry. The famous ferry is the only way to cross between Staten Island and Manhattan without a vehicle. The five-mile ride takes twenty-five minutes and gives you one of the best views of New York Harbor. At night, the ride can be somewhat romantic and can make for a great date. The Staten Island Ferry is one of the last ferries remaining from an entire ferry system in New York City. Every day, seventy-thousand passengers ride the Staten Island Ferry between Staten Island and Lower Manhattan. This number does not include weekend passengers. Annually, over 22 million people ride the ferry.

Since its founding in 2005, Salvatore Bklyn has become the ricotta cheese in New York City. Unfortunately, it's not vegan. Our vegan version, made with tofu, is just as rich and creamy as theirs. Try it in our Lasagna (page 86) or simply mix some into a batch of pasta with tomato sauce for a rich treat.

TOFU RICOTTA

Makes 3 cups

1 (14-ounce) container extra-firm tofu, drained and rinsed
2 teaspoons fresh lemon juice
1 clove garlic, minced
2 tablespoons finely chopped fresh basil
1/2 teaspoon salt
Ground black pepper, to taste
1 tablespoon extra-virgin olive oil
1/4 cup nutritional yeast

1. In a large bowl, mash the tofu until it is thoroughly crumbled. Add the lemon juice, garlic, basil, salt, and pepper. Mash and stir the ingredients until well combined.

2. Add the olive oil and nutritional yeast. Mix well. Cover and refrigerate the ricotta until ready to use.

Many of the commercially available vegan meats rely on soy as a base. Our homemade vegan ham is both gluten-free and soy-free, so everybody can ham it up and nobody gets hurt. These slices work great in our Tofu Benedict (page 34).

RICE PAPER HAM

Makes 4 slices

1 tablespoon tamari
1 teaspoon maple syrup
1/8 teaspoon garlic powder
1/8 teaspoon paprika
2 teaspoons water
4 sheets rice paper

1. Combine the tamari, maple syrup, garlic powder, paprika, and water in a shallow bowl or cake pan.

2. Stack 2 sheets of rice paper and run them quickly under warm water. They should become pliable and stick together. Dip them into the tamari marinade and set aside. Repeat with the remaining 2 sheets of rice paper.

3. Heat a medium nonstick skillet over medium-high heat and spray lightly with nonstick cooking spray. Add one stack of marinated rice paper to the skillet and cook for 30 seconds. Flip it over and cook for 30 seconds. Remove the rice paper from the skillet and transfer it to a plate. Repeat with the other stack of rice paper. Cut each stack in half and the fold each half in half so you end up with 4 rounded triangles.

"To Europe she was America. To America she was the gateway to the earth. But to tell the story of New York would be to write a social history of the world."

— H. G. Wells

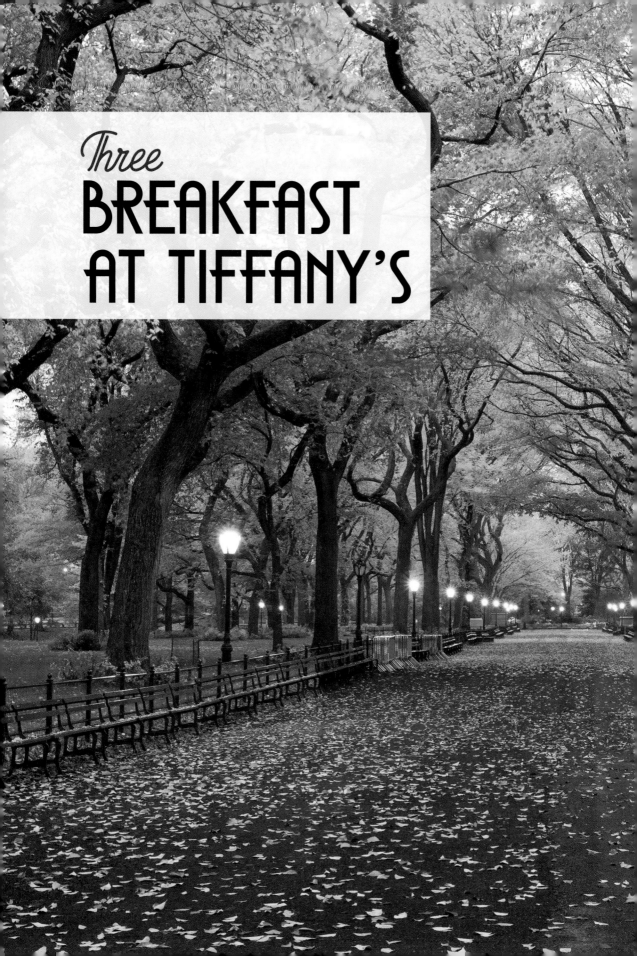

Three
BREAKFAST
AT TIFFANY'S

Whether you only have a New York minute and need a quick grab 'n' go meal like a bagel and coffee from your corner deli, or you have time for a leisurely Sunday brunch with the *New York Times*, we've got you covered. When you consider that New York City is "the city that never sleeps," it seems a little odd to have a section specifically for breakfast. However, in New York City, breakfast is not necessarily the first meal of the day: if you are finishing an overnight shift at work, breakfast might be your dinner, or, after a night of dancing, you might want to get some pancakes at 3:00 a.m. to prevent a hangover. Thankfully, in New York City, you can always find breakfast somewhere, no matter what time of the day or night.

Michael: *Pancakes are the first thing I ever cooked on my own. One morning when I was seven years old, my mom asked me what I wanted for breakfast. "Pancakes," I replied. She took out her 1961 edition of the New York Times Cookbook, opened it to page 486 and said, "Okay, here you go." And that is how I learned to cook. For years, that was my go-to pancake recipe. The pancakes from that recipe were very thin, unlike pancakes from New York City diners, which are anything but thin. This recipe makes big, thick, fluffy diner-style pancakes.*

DINER-STYLE PANCAKES

Makes 12 pancakes

2 cups Chock Full o' Nuts Milk (page 7) or store-bought nondairy milk
2 teaspoons apple cider vinegar
3 tablespoons canola oil or other neutral oil
1 teaspoon vanilla extract
2 cups unbleached all-purpose flour (or gluten-free flour)
1/2 teaspoon baking soda
1 teaspoon baking powder
1 teaspoon salt
2 teaspoons sugar
1/4 teaspoon xanthan gum (only if making gluten-free pancakes)
2 cups nondairy chocolate chips or fresh fruit (such as blueberries, sliced strawberries, or sliced bananas), optional

1. In a medium bowl, combine the milk and vinegar. Mix well and set aside to thicken for 5 minutes. Whisk the oil and vanilla into the milk mixture.

2. In a large bowl, whisk together the flour, baking soda, baking powder, salt, sugar, and xanthan gum (if using to make gluten-free). Pour the milk mixture on top of the flour mixture and whisk just until the batter is just blended. Don't overmix it—a few lumps are fine.

3. Heat an electric griddle or frying pan to 350°F. Spray the griddle with nonstick cooking spray. Gently ladle 1/4 cup of the batter onto the griddle and sprinkle on some chocolate chips or fruit (if using). When bubbles begin to set around the edges of the pancake, about 2 minutes, flip the pancake. Cook 2 to 3 minutes on the other side. Repeat this process until all the batter is used.

4. Serve the pancakes immediately or place them on a towel-lined baking sheet and cover them with another towel. Hold the pancakes in a warm place for 20 to 30 minutes.

Note: We've included directions for making these both regular and gluten-free. Use the xanthan gum only if you are making them gluten-free.

Tip: Using a large ice cream scoop works great for ladling the batter onto the griddle.

Bring a Katz's Delicatessen classic to your breakfast table with our vegan cheese blintzes. Once you've made the crêpes, you could fill them with anything you want. But as New Yorkers, we know they simply must be made into cheese blintzes. Okay, maybe potato blintzes, but if you're gonna do that, leave out the sugar and the vanilla from the crêpe. (Yeah, that's a mistake you only make once.)

CHEESE BLINTZES

Makes 24 blintzes

Crêpes:
1 cup Chock Full o' Nuts Milk (page 7) or store-bought nondairy milk
2 cups water, divided
1/2 cup nondairy butter, melted, plus more for frying
2 cups unbleached all-purpose flour
1/2 teaspoon salt
2 tablespoons sugar
1 tablespoon vanilla extract

Sweet Cheese Filling:
1 (14-ounce) block firm tofu, drained, rinsed, and pressed for 1 hour
1 (8-ounce) container nondairy cream cheese, softened
1 tablespoon nutritional yeast
1/4 cup granulated sugar
1 teaspoon salt

For Serving:
Confectioners' sugar, for dusting
Blueberry Sauce (page 26)

1. **Crêpes:** In a blender, combine the milk, 1 3/4 cups of the water, butter, flour, salt, sugar, and vanilla. Blend until fully mixed. The batter should be very runny. If it is too thick, add the remaining 1/4 cup water. Let the batter rest for 30 minutes.

2. Heat an 8-inch crêpe pan or nonstick pan over medium heat and brush it with a little melted butter. Pour 1/4 cup of batter into the pan and swirl it around so it covers the bottom evenly; pour any excess back into the remaining batter. Cook for 30 to 45 seconds, until the batter sets. Use a heat-proof rubber spatula to loosen and flip the crêpe. Cook another 30 seconds. The crêpes should be pliable, not crisp, and lightly brown. Slide them onto a plate and continue making the crêpes until all the batter is used. Cover the stack of crêpes with a towel to keep them from drying out.

3. **Sweet Cheese Filling:** Crumble the tofu into a medium mixing bowl. Add the cream cheese and mix together well. Your hands are the best tools for the job. Add the nutritional yeast, sugar, and salt. Mix well to thoroughly combine. Taste and add more sugar or salt as needed. The mixture should taste like sweet cheese, slightly sweet and a bit salty.

4. **Fill and fry the crêpes:** Spoon 2 tablespoons of the sweet cheese filling along the lower third of the crêpe. Fold the bottom edge of the crêpe away from you to just cover the filling. Then, fold the 2 sides in to the center. Roll the crêpe away from you a couple of times to make a package, ending with the seam side down. Repeat this process with the remaining crêpes.

Heat a medium skillet over medium heat. Add a little butter to the skillet. Pan-fry the blintzes for 2 minutes per side until crisp and golden. Remove the blintzes from the skillet and drain them on a paper towel–lined plate. Repeat this process until all the blintzes are fried. To serve, dust the blintzes with confectioners' sugar and serve with the blueberry sauce.

BLUEBERRY SAUCE

Makes 3 1/2 cups

This simple blueberry sauce tastes great over Diner-Style Pancakes (page 22), Cheese Blintzes (page 24), or even Chocolate Chip Ice Cream (page 162). If you don't like blueberries, try using strawberries, blackberries, or raspberries. You can even use a mixture of berries rather than just one kind. If you don't like berries, well then, you're on your own.

  1 cup water
  1 cup sugar
  3 cups fresh or frozen blueberries

1. Combine the water and sugar in a medium saucepan over medium-high heat and bring to a simmer. When it beings to simmer, reduce the heat to medium and allow the mixture to simmer 5 minutes, until the sugar is dissolved.

2. Add the blueberries and simmer 5 more minutes. Serve the blueberry sauce warm over hot foods, like cheese blintzes, or serve cold over ice cream. Store any leftovers covered in the refrigerator for up to 1 week.

"What, indeed, is a New Yorker? Is he Jew or Irish? Is he English or German? Is he Russian or Polish? He may be something of all these, and yet he is wholly none of them. . . . New York, indeed, resembles a magic cauldron. Those who are cast into it are born again."

— Charles Whibley, *American Sketches*

This recipe was inspired by one of our favorite restaurants in New York City, Sacred Chow. One of the tastiest items on its amazing brunch menu is the Banana French Toast: battered slices of banana pound cake cooked on a griddle. We made our own version using homemade Banana Bread (page 163).

BANANA BREAD FRENCH TOAST

Serves 4

1 1/2 cups Chock Full o' Nuts Milk (page 7) or store-bought nondairy milk
1 cup unbleached all-purpose flour
2 tablespoons maple syrup, plus more for serving
1 tablespoon vanilla extract
8 slices Banana Bread (page 163)
Confectioners' sugar, for serving, optional
Blueberry Sauce (page 26), optional

1. Heat a griddle over medium heat. Combine the milk, flour, maple syrup, and vanilla in a medium bowl. Mix well so that there are no lumps of flour. Pour the batter into a shallow dish. We like using a cake pan.

2. Lightly spray the griddle with nonstick cooking spray or brush lightly with some oil. One at a time, put a slice of the banana bread into the batter, to coat one side. Flip it over to coat the other side. Carefully lift it out of the batter and allow any excess to drip back into the pan. Place the bread onto the griddle and repeat the process with the remaining slices of bread.

3. Cook the bread 2 to 3 minutes on the first side, or until lightly browned. Flip and cook 2 to 3 minutes longer on the other side. Serve the French toast with additional maple syrup, a dusting of confectioners' sugar, or blueberry sauce.

Irish immigrants were among the earliest immigrants to the Big Apple. This recipe is our NYC take on a traditional Irish breakfast of oatmeal. We combine old-fashioned oats with applesauce to make an easy apple pie–flavored breakfast.

BIG APPLE OATMEAL

Makes 1 serving

1/2 cup old-fashioned rolled oats (do not use quick-cooking or instant oats)
1/2 cup boiling water
1/2 cup unsweetened applesauce
1/4 teaspoon ground cinnamon
1/8 teaspoon ground nutmeg

1. Place the oats in a microwave-safe bowl and pour the water over them. Use a spoon and press the oats down into the hot water to make sure all of the oats are wet. Let them soak for 3 to 4 minutes.

2. Once the oats have absorbed most of the water, place them in the microwave on high for 1 1/2 to 2 minutes. Cooking times and strengths are different on each microwave, so there might be some variation here. When the oats are done, they should look a bit pasty and there should be no water left at all. Add the applesauce, cinnamon, and nutmeg. Mix well to incorporate. Microwave again for 30 seconds. Let cool slightly and eat.

Stopping into a local deli or bodega on your way to work to grab a ham, egg, and cheese on a roll is a routine for many New Yorkers. You can make a vegan version of this sandwich just as easily. For a true New York City experience, make one for someone else, ask them if they want salt and pepper on it, and, regardless of the answer, add the salt and pepper. We list ketchup as being optional, but for Ethan it is required.

BREAKFAST SANDWICH

Serves 2

1 (14-ounce) block firm tofu, drained and rinsed
1/4 teaspoon black salt
1/8 teaspoon turmeric
2 slices nondairy American cheese
2 round sandwich rolls, sliced in half
2 slices Rice Paper Ham (page 18) or store-bought vegan ham
Salt and ground black pepper, to taste
Ketchup, optional

1. Cut the tofu in half lengthwise to get 2 (1-inch) slabs. Use a round biscuit cutter or a glass to cut a large circle out of each piece that is slightly smaller than the sandwich rolls.

2. Mix together the black salt and turmeric in a small bowl and then rub the mixture onto both pieces of tofu. Set the tofu aside for 5 minutes. Place 1 slice of cheese on the bottom half of each roll. Set aside.

3. Spray a medium skillet with nonstick cooking spray and heat over medium-high heat. Add the tofu rounds and cook on one side until lightly browned, about 3 minutes. Flip and cook on the other side for 3 more minutes. Remove the tofu from the skillet and place one round on top of each slice of cheese.

4. Return the skillet to the heat and cook the vegan ham slices for 15 seconds on each side. You just want to heat them up. Place the vegan ham on top of the tofu rounds. Sprinkle with the salt and pepper and add some ketchup (if using). Add a top of the roll to each sandwich and serve.

Frittatas are very popular items on New York City brunch menus. We give ours the classic American flavor combination of bacon, broccoli, and cheddar. This frittata comes across as complex, but is actually very easy to make. It's a great make-ahead dish: you can prepare it on Saturday, put in the refrigerator overnight, stay out late with friends, roll out of bed Sunday morning, and pop it in the oven just before your brunch guests arrive.

BACON, BROCCOLI, AND CHEDDAR FRITTATA

Serves 4 to 6

4 ounces tempeh bacon
2 teaspoons canola oil or other neutral oil
1 small onion, cut into 1/4-inch pieces
2 cups coarsely chopped fresh broccoli florets
1/4 cup plus 2 tablespoons water, divided
1 tablespoon arrowroot powder or cornstarch
1 (14-ounce) block firm tofu, drained and rinsed
1/8 teaspoon turmeric
2 tablespoons nutritional yeast
Salt and ground black pepper, to taste
1/4 cup shredded nondairy cheddar cheese

1. Preheat the oven to 375°F. Lightly spray a 9-inch round baking pan with nonstick cooking spray. Set aside. Spray a nonstick medium skillet with nonstick cooking spray and heat over medium-high heat. Add the tempeh bacon and cook until lightly browned, about 2 minutes. Flip the tempeh bacon and cook on the other side for another minute. Remove the tempeh bacon from the skillet, cut into 1/2-inch pieces, and put it into a large mixing bowl.

2. In the same skillet, heat the oil over medium-high heat. Add the onion, toss to coat it with oil, and cover the skillet. Cook for 5 minutes, or until the onion is soft. Add the broccoli and 1/4 cup of water to the skillet, cover, and cook until the broccoli is soft, about 5 minutes. Remove the lid and cook to allow any remaining water to evaporate. Add the onion mixture to the bowl with the tempeh bacon and toss to evenly distribute the onion, broccoli, and tempeh bacon.

3. In a small bowl, stir together the arrowroot and the remaining 2 tablespoons of water until there are no lumps. Add the tofu, arrowroot mixture, turmeric, and nutritional yeast to a food processor and process until smooth. Season with the salt and pepper.

4. Transfer the tofu mixture to the bowl with the tempeh bacon mixture. Add the cheese and mix well. Transfer the mixture to the prepared baking pan. Bake until the tofu is set and the top is golden brown, about 35 minutes. Remove the frittata from the oven and allow it to cool slightly before serving.

No breakfast section in a vegan cookbook would be complete without a tofu scramble. We give ours an Italian twist with tomatoes and basil. Serve this with an espresso and some toasted Italian bread and it's just like having breakfast in Little Italy, only better.

ITALIAN TOFU SCRAMBLE

Serves 4

2 teaspoons extra-virgin olive oil
1 clove garlic, minced
1 (14-ounce) container soft tofu, drained and rinsed
1 cup diced tomatoes, fresh or drained canned
1/2 teaspoon salt
1/2 teaspoon dried oregano
1/4 cup fresh basil, minced

Heat the oil in a large skillet over medium heat. Add the garlic and sauté for 30 seconds. Crumble the tofu and add it to the skillet and sauté for 1 minute. Add the tomatoes and their juice to the tofu and fold them together. Add the salt, oregano, and basil and mix well. Cook an additional 1 minute to cook off any liquid and to heat through.

Irish Influence

One of the most significant ethnic groups in all of New York City is the Irish. Over half a million New Yorkers are of Irish ancestry. The Irish have been in New York since pre-Colonial times, back when the City was still called New Amsterdam. But the really large wave of immigration happened in the mid-nineteenth century when the Great Irish Famine forced over 1.5 million people out of Ireland. There are many longstanding, well-established Irish communities in all five boroughs, notably including Hell's Kitchen in Manhattan. The oldest Irish Pub in New York is McSorely's Old Ale House, on East 7th Street in the East Village, and it has been continuously operating since 1854. New York City has a longstanding tradition of Irish involvement in city politics, the New York City Police Department, the Fire Department, and the Roman Catholic Church.

It is said that everyone in New York City is Irish on St. Patrick's Day. Bagels are dyed green, pastries are filled with green cream and, of course, the beer is green. You can make your soda bread green if you want; however, we like the rich yellow color it gets just on its own.

IRISH SODA BREAD

Makes 1 loaf

2 tablespoons apple cider vinegar
14 ounces plain unsweetened nondairy milk
450 grams (about 3 cups) unbleached all-purpose flour
1 teaspoon baking soda
1 teaspoon salt

1. Preheat the oven to 450°F. Line an 18 x 12-inch baking sheet with parchment and set aside

2. In a small bowl, mix together the vinegar and milk. Set aside for 5 minutes to curdle.

3. In a large bowl, whisk together the flour, baking soda, and salt. Make a well in the center of the flour mixture. Pour in the milk mixture, and, starting in the center, use your hand to mix it together, working from the inside out. You can use a wooden spoon, but your hand really does a better job. It should only take a few moments for all the flour to be incorporated. Do not overmix.

4. Put the dough on a lightly floured work surface and gently gather it into a ball about 7 inches in diameter. You don't want to knead it, just bring it all together.

5. Place the dough ball on the prepared baking sheet. Using a serrated knife, cut a large "X" into the dough, about 1/4-inch deep. This will help the rising. Then, using the tip of your knife, prick each of the 4 sections of the dough. This is an Irish tradition and is supposed to "let the faeries escape." (Legend holds that if you don't do this, the faeries will jinx your bread and it will be tough.)

6. Bake the bread for 20 minutes. After 20 minutes, reduce the heat to 400°F, flip the bread over and bake 15 minutes longer. After 15 minutes, flip the bread over again and bake 5 more minutes. If your bread is getting too dark, tent it with some aluminum foil.

7. Remove the bread from the oven and serve warm. To serve the bread, break the loaf in half with your hands and put out the halves.

Nothing says Sunday brunch quite like Tofu Benedict. The infamous nonvegan version of this brunch classic was created in New York City in the 1890s, but there are competing myths about its exact origin. One story says it was created at Delmonico's circa 1892 for Mrs. LeGrand Benedict, while the other says it was created in 1894 at the Waldorf-Astoria for Mr. Lemeul Benedict. Whichever story is true, we're sure glad the Benedicts had someone to whip up this winning flavor combo.

TOFU BENEDICT

Serves 4

2 (14-ounce) containers firm tofu, drained, rinsed, and sliced lengthwise into 4 slabs
1/2 cup tamari
4 tablespoons water
1/4 cup agave nectar
4 English muffins, sliced in half (use gluten-free muffins for a gluten-free option)
2 tablespoons canola oil or other neutral oil, divided
8 slices Rice Paper Ham (page 18) or tempeh bacon
Hollandaise Sauce (page 82)

1. Place the tofu slabs in a shallow baking dish in a single layer. In a small bowl, combine the tamari, water, and agave. Mix well and pour over the tofu. Set the tofu aside for 30 minutes to marinate.

2. Toast the muffins until golden brown and crisp. While the muffins are toasting, add 1 tablespoon of the oil to a large skillet and heat over medium heat. Arrange the tofu in the skillet, working in batches if needed, and sear the slabs on one side for 3 minutes, or until lightly golden. Flip the tofu and sear on the other side for 3 minutes. Remove the tofu slabs from the skillet and place them on a paper towel–lined plate to absorb any excess oil. Add the remaining 1 tablespoon oil to the skillet and sear the ham slices on each side for 10 seconds.

3. Arrange two muffin halves, cut-side up, on each of four plates. Top each muffin half with one slice of the ham. Place one piece of the tofu on top of each ham slice. Ladle the Hollandaise sauce generously over each portion and serve.

Variation: Replace the vegan ham with sautéed spinach for tofu Florentine.

Matzoh is the unleavened flatbread that Jews eat over the eight days of Passover. Matzoh brei (meaning "fried matzo") is often considered a Passover version of French toast. A few restaurants, like B&H on Manhattan's Lower East Side, serve it all year-round. Some people prefer their matzoh brei savory, but we prefer it sweet. To make it savory, simply leave out the maple syrup and add some sautéed onions.

MATZOH BREI

Serves 4

5 sheets matzoh
7 ounces silken tofu
2 tablespoons nondairy butter, melted
2 tablespoons maple syrup, plus more for serving
1/2 cup Chock Full o' Nuts Milk (page 7) or store-bought nondairy milk
1 tablespoon Ener-G Egg Replacer or cornstarch
1/2 teaspoon salt
Ketchup, for serving

1. Place the matzoh in a large mixing bowl and break the sheets into large pieces. Cover the matzoh pieces with water and let them soak for 5 minutes, or until the matzoh is soggy.

2. In a blender, combine the tofu, butter, maple syrup, milk, egg replacer, and salt. Blend until completely smooth.

3. Drain the matzoh and squeeze out as much water as possible. Return the matzoh to the mixing bowl. Add the tofu mixture to the matzoh and mix well.

4. Heat a large skillet over medium-high heat, spray it with nonstick cooking spray, and add the matzoh mixture. Sauté until slightly brown and crispy on the edges, about 7 minutes. Serve the matzoh brei with ketchup or additional maple syrup, depending on whether you prefer it sweet or savory.

Streit's Matzoh

Streit's Matzoh, the only family-owned matzoh company in the United States, was started in New York City in 1916 by Aaron Streit. It continued operating on Manhattan's Lower East Side until 2007, when the factory was sold and operations moved out of the city. The Lower East Side is the area between Bowery Street on the west, the FDR Drive on the east, East Houston Street to the north, and Canal Street to the south. During the late nineteenth and early twentieth centuries, the Lower East Side was the home for Jewish immigrants to the United States. While this neighborhood was once filled with synagogues and historic buildings, gentrification has erased most of them as this area is now a home to many bars and clubs. To get a taste of the old Lower East Side, visit the Tenement Museum at 103 Orchard Street.

Michael: I came up with this recipe when our aging dog, Phoebe, was getting finicky about eating. In addition to being picky about how she wanted her food, she decided that not only was I the only one allowed to feed her but Ethan couldn't even be in the kitchen when I fed her. Her morning feedings could often take upward of twenty minutes, so I didn't have time to sit down and eat a traditional breakfast. I needed something quick and started making this breakfast smoothie. Even though Phoebe has since passed, I still enjoy this quick, nutrient-dense breakfast—and I enjoy all of the extra time before work.

FRUIT SMOOTHIE

Makes 1 smoothie

4 ounces silken tofu
1 large orange, peeled and seeded
1/3 cup fresh or frozen blueberries
5 fresh or frozen strawberries, hulled
1 medium banana
1/2 fresh large peach, cut into six wedges or 1 cup frozen peach slices

1. Combine all the ingredients in a blender. Blend until smooth.

2. Pour the smoothie into a tall glass and serve.

The nonstop energy of New York City can often be draining to those of us who live here. A Green Smoothie is the perfect way to give yourself just the right boost of energy to help you face the hustle and bustle of everyday life here.

GREEN SMOOTHIE

Makes 1 smoothie

1 cup frozen pineapple chunks
1 medium banana, frozen
1 cup spinach, loosely packed
1 cup coconut water

1. Combine all the ingredients in a blender. Blend until smooth.

2. Pour the smoothie into a tall glass and serve.

On weekday mornings in New York City, coffee carts pop up on corners everywhere. In addition to the classic cup of joe, they serve bagels, doughnuts, and cinnamon rolls. Vegans in New York know that they can get vegan cinnamon rolls at Erin McKenna's bakery (formerly known as Babycakes) or the famous Cinnamon Snail at The Pennsy. When it's too cold to schlep outside for one of theirs, we make these at home, pour ourselves a big cup of coffee, and wait for spring.

CINNAMON ROLLS

Makes 8 rolls

Cinnamon Rolls:
4 tablespoons nondairy butter, melted
3 tablespoons granulated sugar, divided
1 1/2 tablespoons ground cinnamon, divided
1 pound Pizza Dough (page 8) or store-bought vegan pizza dough

Frosting:
1/4 cup confectioners' sugar
1 tablespoon water
4 tablespoons nondairy butter, at room temperature
1 ounce nondairy cream cheese, at room temperature

1. Preheat the oven to 350°F. In a small bowl, stir together the melted butter, 2 tablespoons of the granulated sugar, and 1 tablespoon of the cinnamon.

2. In a separate small bowl, combine the remaining 1 tablespoon granulated sugar and 1/2 tablespoon cinnamon and set aside.

3. On a lightly floured surface, lightly roll out the pizza dough into a 1/4-inch thick rectangle. Brush the butter mixture evenly across the dough. Starting with one of the shorter sides, roll the dough up into a jelly roll. Using a knife or pizza cutter, cut the roll into 8 equally sized pieces.

4. Grease an 8 x 8-inch baking dish or 8-inch round cake pan and arrange the cinnamon rolls evenly. Sprinkle with the reserved cinnamon sugar mixture. Bake the rolls for 17 to 18 minutes.

5. Remove the rolls from the oven and allow them to cool slightly before frosting.

6. While the rolls are cooling, make the frosting. In a medium bowl, whisk together the confectioners' sugar and water until smooth. Add the butter and cream cheese and beat with a hand mixer until smooth and creamy, about 30 seconds. Frost the cinnamon rolls.

7. Store leftover rolls in a covered container for up to 3 days in the refrigerator. Reheat them in the microwave before serving to freshen them up.

Paris may have croissants and baguettes, but New York City has bagels. Bagels first arrived in New York City with the Eastern European migration of the late 1800s. By 1910, there were so many bagel makers in the city that a bagel bakers' union was formed. To make truly authentic New York City bagels, you have to boil them before baking them to achieve their signature dense texture and chewy crust.

NEW YORK-STYLE BAGELS

Makes 8 bagels

1 1/4 cups warm water (110°F to 115°F), divided
2 teaspoons active dry yeast
1 1/2 tablespoons sugar
3 1/2 cups bread flour
Pinch salt

1. Mix 1/2 cup of the warm water with the yeast and sugar in a small measuring cup. Set aside until it starts to bubble, about 5 minutes. If it does not bubble, the yeast is not active. Get new yeast and start over.

2. In a large mixing bowl, combine the flour and salt. Add the yeast mixture to the flour mixture and stir with a wooden spoon. Pour half of the 3/4 cup remaining water into the flour mixture. Knead with your hands, adding additional water to moisten the dough as needed. The dough should be neither dry nor wet.

3. Transfer the dough to a well-floured work surface. Knead the dough for 15 to 20 minutes, or until smooth and elastic. You can also do this in a stand mixer with a dough hook.

4. Place the dough in an oiled mixing bowl and cover it with a damp towel or plastic wrap. Let the dough rise in a warm place for about 1 hour. Punch it down and let it rest another 10 minutes.

5. Divide the dough into 8 pieces and shape each one into a ball. On a floured work surface, roll the dough until very smooth and perfectly round. Gently press a finger into the center of the dough to make a bagel shape. Work the hole until it has a 3/4-inch diameter, about the size of a quarter. Place the bagel on a parchment-lined baking sheet. Repeat with the remaining dough balls. Cover the bagels with a damp towel and let them rest for 15 to 20 minutes. While the bagels are resting, preheat the oven to 400°F.

6. Bring a large pot of water to a rapid boil. Reduce the heat to a simmer and place 3 or 4 bagels in the water using a slotted spoon. Do not crowd them. After a few seconds, they should float to the top of the water. If they don't, loosen them from the bottom of the pot with a spoon. Once the bagels float to the top, flip them over and simmer for 1 minute. Remove the bagels with a slotted spoon and return them to the baking sheet. (See Note below.) Repeat until all the bagels are boiled.

7. Place the baking sheet in the oven and bake the bagels for about 20 minutes or until golden brown. Remove them from the oven and transfer them to a wire rack to cool. Store in a plastic bag for up to 3 days on the counter or 5 days in the refrigerator.

Note: To make sesame, poppy, or everything bagels, place your desired topping on a plate and when the bagels come out of the water, press the bagels into the topping.

Four
POWER
LUNCH

Lunchtime options in New York are as diverse and varied at the City itself. Whether you eat at your desk or enjoy a full lunch hour, treating yourself to a great lunch is something everyone should do for themselves. In the warm months, many restaurants set up outdoor seating, allowing people to enjoy fresh air while they take their lunch. The emergence of food trucks throughout the City has increased the lunch options available. Some of the trucks move around during the week and update diners daily via social media as to where they will be on any given day. Whether you're taking lunch out, stopping at a food truck, bringing it from home, or going to a formal lunch meeting at a restaurant, most lunch options include soups, salads, or sandwiches. Here are some New York City classics.

When we first met, one of the things we bonded over was our love for the movie My Big Fat Greek Wedding. Even today, we still quote lines from it to one another when the situation calls for it. Before we became vegan, one of our favorite Greek places to eat in New York City was Uncle Nick's in the Theatre District. The restaurant was loud, crowded, and always fun to visit. Michael's favorite thing on the menu was the avgolemono soup—chicken soup with lemon and rice. Our vegan version is even better than Uncle Nick's. For a gluten-free version, replace the seitan with Chicken-Style Soy Curls (page 14).

AVGOLEMONO SOUP

Serves 4 to 6

4 cups vegetable broth
1/4 cup long-grain white rice
3 tablespoons nutritional yeast
2 teaspoons tamari
1 cup plain unsweetened soymilk or other milk
2 tablespoons cornstarch
1/4 teaspoon ground turmeric
1/3 cup Chicken-Style Seitan (page 12), cut into 1/4-inch dice
1 tablespoon extra-virgin olive oil
1/3 cup fresh lemon juice, divided
1 tablespoon lemon zest
1/4 cup finely chopped fresh parsley
Salt and ground black pepper, to taste

1. In a large pot, combine the vegetable broth, rice, nutritional yeast, and tamari. Bring to a boil, then lower the heat, cover the pot, and simmer for 25 minutes, until the rice is cooked.

2. While the rice is cooking, combine the soymilk, cornstarch, and turmeric in a small bowl. Mix with a fork and set aside.

3. When the rice is cooked, re-stir the soymilk mixture and add it to the soup. Stir until the soup has thickened. Add the seitan, oil, 1/4 cup of the lemon juice, and lemon zest to the soup. Mix well and taste the soup for tartness. If you like it more tart, add the remaining lemon juice. Add the parsley and salt and pepper. Stir well. Serve hot.

For old-world Italian food in New York City, head to Arthur Avenue in the Bronx. Though eating there as a vegan can be challenging, our minestrone will make you feel like you are sitting in an Italian grandmother's kitchen.

MINESTRONE SOUP

Serves 6

2 tablespoons extra-virgin olive oil
1 large onion, cut into 1/4-inch pieces
4 cloves garlic, minced
1 cup thinly sliced savoy cabbage
2 celery ribs, cut into 1/4-inch pieces
1 large carrot, cut into 1/4-inch pieces
1 teaspoon dried oregano
3 tablespoons finely chopped fresh basil, divided
3/4 teaspoon salt, plus more as needed
1/4 teaspoon ground black pepper
1 (28-ounce) can diced tomatoes, undrained
1 (14-ounce) can crushed tomatoes
6 cups low-sodium vegetable broth
1 dried bay leaf
1 (15-ounce) can kidney beans, drained and rinsed
1 (15-ounce) can cannellini beans, drained and rinsed
1 cup dried elbow pasta or cut fusilli

1. Heat the oil in a large pot over medium-high heat. Add the onion and cook until translucent, about 4 minutes. Add the garlic and cook 30 seconds. Add the cabbage, celery, and carrot to the pot and stir well. Cook, stirring often, until the vegetables begin to soften, about 5 minutes.

2. Stir in the oregano, 1 tablespoon of the basil, salt, and pepper. Cook for 3 more minutes. Add the diced tomatoes, crushed tomatoes, vegetable broth, and bay leaf to the pot, stir well, and bring the soup to a boil. Reduce the heat to medium-low and simmer for 10 minutes.

3. Stir in the kidney beans, cannellini beans, and pasta. Cook until the pasta and vegetables are tender, about 10 minutes. Season with additional salt, if needed. Remove and discard the bay leaf. Ladle the soup into bowls and top with the remaining chopped basil.

Because kitchen space is at premium in New York City, this soup is particularly great as it doesn't require a lot of prep room. If you can open a can, you can make this soup. Serve this with a nice, crusty Italian bread and some chianti for a light Italian meal.

TUSCAN WHITE BEAN SOUP

Serves 6

2 teaspoons extra-virgin olive oil
2 cloves garlic, minced
2 (15-ounce) cans cannellini beans, drained and rinsed
1 teaspoon fresh rosemary, minced
6 cups vegetable broth
1 (14-ounce) can diced tomatoes, drained
1 tablespoon salt
2 teaspoons ground black pepper

1. Heat the oil in a large pot over medium-high heat. Add the garlic and sauté for 30 seconds or until fragrant. Add the beans, rosemary, vegetable broth, tomatoes, salt, and pepper to the pot, stirring well to combine. Bring the soup to a boil, then reduce the heat to a simmer for 30 minutes. Taste the soup for seasoning. Add more salt and pepper if desired. You can stop here and have a light, broth-based soup with lots of beans or go one step further for a heartier soup.

2. Use an immersion blender and puree the soup a little bit to break down some of the beans and thicken the soup. You don't want to puree the entire soup. Leave plenty of beans whole. If you don't have an immersion blender, you can use a potato masher to mash some of the beans or scoop out some of the beans, broth, and tomatoes, put them into a blender, blend for a few seconds, then stir this puree back into the remaining soup.

Little Italy

Nonnative New Yorkers think of Little Italy on Manhattan's Mulberry Street as the place to go for authentic Italian food in New York. In truth, this Little Italy is really just a big tourist trap. Real New Yorkers know that Arthur Avenue in the Belmont section of the Bronx is the real Little Italy. Italian immigrants settled here and established a vibrant community back in the 1950s. Interestingly, the highest population of Italian Americans of any county in the United States is in Staten Island. As you can see, you can find lots of Italian food in neighborhoods throughout the five boroughs, ensuring that you are never far from great Italian food in New York City.

For vegans dining with omnivores in New York City, going to a Japanese restaurant is often a great choice as there is always something vegan on the menu. While the East Village and Midtown East have accumulated large concentrations of Japanese restaurants, you can find Japanese restaurants in just about every neighborhood. The base or "dashi" in most miso soups uses bonito flakes made from fish. This vegan dashi, the base of our hearty soup, can also be used in a wide variety of Japanese dishes.

MISO VEGETABLE SOUP

Serves 6

8 cups water
2 pieces kombu
2 tablespoons low-sodium soy sauce or tamari
3 dried shiitake mushrooms
1 large carrot, peeled and sliced into 1/8-inch thick rounds
1/2 medium daikon radish, sliced into 1/8-inch thick half-moons
1 clove garlic, minced
2 yellow potatoes, cut into 1/2-inch pieces
7 ounces firm tofu, drained, pressed, and cut into 1/4-inch pieces
1/4 cup dried wakame
6 tablespoons mellow white miso
2 green onions, finely chopped

1. To make the dashi, in a large pot, combine the water, kombu, soy sauce, and shiitake mushrooms. Bring this mixture to a rolling boil, cover, and cook for 5 minutes.

2. Add the carrot, daikon, garlic, and potatoes. Stir well, cover the pot, and bring back to a boil. Lower the heat to medium and cook for 10 minutes. Remove and discard the kombu. Lower the heat to a simmer and stir in the tofu and wakame.

3. Ladle 2 cups of the liquid into a medium mixing bowl. Add the miso to the bowl and stir and mash with a fork until fully dissolved. Pour the miso mixture into the soup and stir well.

4. Allow the soup to simmer 5 minutes longer but be careful not to allow it to boil, as boiling will change the texture and taste of the miso. Turn off the heat, ladle the soup into bowls and top each portion with the green onions.

Ethan: *Known to many as Jewish penicillin, chicken soup is a staple in diners and kosher delis throughout New York City. My Hungarian grandmother would always serve her soup with radishes. Simply wash and slice them in half, salt the cut ends and take a bite before each spoonful.*

NEW-FASHIONED JEWISH CHICK'N SOUP

Serves 6

1 teaspoon extra-virgin olive oil
2 medium sweet onions, cut into 1/4-inch pieces
1 teaspoon sea salt
1/4 teaspoon ground black pepper
3 cloves garlic, minced
3 cloves garlic, roughly chopped
2 rounded teaspoons vegan chicken bouillon paste or 2 vegan chicken bouillon cubes
2 large carrots, sliced into 1/4-inch thick rounds
2 celery ribs, cut into 1/4-inch pieces
8 cups vegetable broth, divided
2 cups boiling water
Additions: Cooked noodles, cooked rice, cubed pressed tofu

1. Heat the oil in a large pot over medium-high heat. Add the onions, sea salt, and ground black pepper and sauté until the onions are golden, about 5 minutes. Add the garlic and sauté for 30 seconds, or until fragrant.

2. Lower the heat to medium and add the bouillon paste. Stir to thoroughly coat everything. Add the carrots, celery, and 3/4 cup of the vegetable broth. Scrape the bottom of the pot well to lift up any browned bits, cover, and cook for 3 minutes.

3. Add the remaining 7 1/4 cups vegetable broth and boiling water. Mix well, cover, and bring the soup to a rolling boil. Let it boil for 1 minute before lowering to a high simmer and cook for 1 hour. Stir in your favorite additions. Serve hot.

Sometimes, when we don't have time to pack a lunch to bring to work, we will order something from one of our favorite vegan lunch spots, Terri. Our go-to item at Terri is their Kale Superfood Salad: a bed of kale massaged with a lemon tahini dressing and topped with fresh vegetables and chickpeas. That salad inspired us to make our own version of it at home.

SUPER KALE SALAD WITH LEMON TAHINI DRESSING

Serves 4

1/2 cup tahini
3 tablespoons fresh lemon juice
3/4 cup water
1 clove garlic, minced
2 tablespoons minced fresh parsley
1/2 teaspoon salt
1 large bunch kale, tough stems removed and torn into bite-size pieces (about 5 cups)
1/2 cup cooked quinoa
1 (14-ounce) can chickpeas, drained and rinsed
1/2 cup grape tomatoes, quartered
1 red bell pepper, cut into 1/2-inch pieces
1 yellow bell pepper, cut into 1/2-inch pieces
1 orange bell pepper, cut into 1/2-inch pieces
2 large carrots, shredded
1/2 cup bean or alfalfa sprouts
4 tablespoons Hummus (page 75) or store-bought hummus

1. Combine the tahini, lemon juice, water, garlic, parsley, and salt in a small bowl. Mix until fully combined. Taste and add more salt or lemon juice as needed. If you prefer a thinner dressing, add a little more water.

2. Put the kale in a large bowl. Add 2 tablespoons of the dressing to the kale. Use your hands to massage the dressing into the kale. Divide the kale equally among 4 salad bowls.

3. Place 2 tablespoons of quinoa in the middle of each bowl of kale. Arrange the chickpeas, tomatoes, bell peppers, carrots, sprouts, and hummus around the quinoa in each bowl. Serve the salad with the remaining dressing on the side.

Manhattan clam chowder is the red, tomato-based soup found on diner menus all over the city. We find that mushrooms bring the perfect texture and flavor to this vegan version of the iconic New York City soup.

MANHATTAN GLAM CHOWDER

Serves 8

2 tablespoons extra-virgin olive oil
2 medium carrots, cut into 1/4-inch pieces
2 celery ribs, cut into 1/4-inch pieces
1 medium onion, cut into 1/4-inch pieces
3 cloves garlic, minced
1/4 cup tomato paste
1 teaspoon dried oregano
3 sprigs fresh thyme
2 dried bay leaves
1 tablespoon dulse flakes or 1/2 sheet nori
1 tablespoon Old Bay Seasoning
2 medium waxy potatoes, peeled and cut into 1-inch pieces
8 cups vegetable broth
1 (28-ounce) can whole peeled tomatoes, undrained, coarsely chopped
1 cup diced oyster or cremini mushrooms
8 ounces white button mushrooms, sliced 1/8-inch thick
1/2 cup dry sherry or white wine
2 tablespoons sugar
Salt and ground black pepper, to taste

1. Heat the oil in a large pot over medium heat. Add the carrots, celery, and onion. Cover and cook, stirring occasionally until soft, about 8 minutes. Add the garlic and cook for 1 minute. Stir in the tomato paste and cook, stirring for 1 minute.

2. Add the oregano, thyme, bay leaves, dulse, Old Bay Seasoning, and potatoes. Add the vegetable broth, stir well, and bring the soup to a boil. Reduce the heat to a simmer, cover, and cook until the potatoes are tender, about 10 minutes.

3. Add the tomatoes and stir well. Add the oyster mushrooms, button mushrooms, sherry, and sugar. Bring the soup to a boil again. Cover, reduce the heat, and simmer 10 minutes. Remove and discard the bay leaves, thyme sprigs, and nori (if using). Taste and add salt and pepper as needed. Serve hot.

Oscar Tschirky created this salad sometime between 1893 and 1896 at the Waldorf Hotel, the precursor of the now Waldorf-Astoria Hotel, in Midtown East. While the original recipe didn't contain nuts, we've added walnuts for their taste and because they start with the letter "W."

WALDORF SALAD

Serves 4

1/2 cup nondairy mayonnaise
1 tablespoon sugar
1 teaspoon lemon juice
1/8 teaspoon salt
3 medium Gala, Fuji, or other red sweet apples, peeled, cored, and cut into 1/2-inch pieces
1 cup thinly sliced celery
1/2 cup chopped walnuts
1 cup seedless red grapes, halved

In a medium bowl, whisk together the mayonnaise, sugar, lemon juice, and salt. Stir in the apples, celery, walnuts, and grapes. Chill until ready to serve.

"As for New York City, it is a place apart. There is not its match in any other country in the world."

— Pearl S. Buck

Ethan: *Caprese salad is a staple at Italian restaurants all over New York City. It is said that this salad was made to resemble to colors of the Italian flag, using tomatoes, mozzarella, and basil to provide the signature red, white, and green. I had given up hope that I would ever eat a caprese salad again when I went vegan until I learned to press tofu. Pressing tofu gives it a texture similar to that of buffalo mozzarella. Though historically treated as antipasti, this caprese salad is also a lovely main dish if you're looking to eat lightly, as I often do, on the hot summer evenings.*

CAPRESE SALAD

Serves 4

1 (14-ounce) package extra-firm tofu, drained, rinsed and pressed for 30 minutes
Balsamic vinegar, to taste
Extra-virgin olive oil, to taste
3 medium Roma tomatoes, sliced into 1/4-inch thick rounds
8 to 10 fresh basil leaves, washed and dried
Dried oregano, to taste
Salt, to taste
Ground black pepper, to taste

1. Cut the tofu into even halves. Then cut the two halves evenly in half. Finally, slice each piece in half so that you have 8 rectangular slices.

2. Place the 8 tofu slices in a glass baking pan. Drizzle a few drops of the balsamic vinegar on each rectangle of tofu and rub it in to coat and cover the slice. Flip each slice over and repeat to coat the other side. You should end up with a pretty, marbleized pattern on each piece of tofu.

3. Repeat the above step using the olive oil (again, just drizzle a few drops on each slice, rubbing it in and then doing the same to the second side). Cover the pan with plastic wrap and let the tofu marinate for 20 minutes.

4. Place the marinated tofu on 4 serving plates. Arrange the tomatoes and basil atop the tofu slices. Just before serving, drizzle the salad one last time with a little balsamic vinegar and olive oil, and sprinkle a little oregano, salt, and pepper over each plate.

Variation: Rather than serving this as a layered salad, try dicing the tofu and tomatoes and finely chopping the basil. After the tofu cubes marinade, toss them in a serving bowl with the diced tomatoes and basil. Season with oregano, salt, and pepper and serve.

You cannot walk through a summer street fair in New York City without finding at least one stand selling arepas. These thick cornmeal pancakes came to the city by way of Columbia and Venezuela. They can be eaten on their own or split open and stuffed with your choice of fillings, such as beans, salads, or nondairy cheese.

AREPAS

Makes 8 arepas

1 cup fresh or thawed frozen corn kernels
3/4 cup vegetable broth, warm
1 cup instant cornmeal
1 1/2 teaspoons sugar
1 teaspoon nondairy sour cream
1/4 cup Cashew Parmesan (page 16) or store-bought nondairy Parmesan cheese
1/4 cup canola oil or other neutral oil

1. In a blender, combine the corn kernels and vegetable broth and blend until smooth.

2. Pour the cornmeal into a large bowl. Stir in the sugar and sour cream. Add the corn mixture and mix well to thoroughly combine. Stir in the cashew Parmesan.

3. Form the dough into a ball, then divide it into 8 pieces. Roll each piece into a ball and then flatten into a pancake about 1/4-inch thick and 2 inches in diameter. At this point, you can cover the arepas with a damp kitchen towel and refrigerate them for up to 1 day before frying them.

4. Heat the oil in a large skillet over medium heat. Working in batches, cook the arepas until golden brown, 4 to 5 minutes per side. Transfer the cooked arepas to a paper towel–lined plate to drain until cool enough to handle. They should be golden on the outside but soft in the middle. Let the arepas cool to room temperature.

Ethan: *The iconic Reuben sandwich is named for its creator, Arthur Reuben, the owner of Reuben's Delicatessen in New York City, who started serving them around 1914. Arthur's sandwich was made with corned beef, Swiss cheese, and sauerkraut and served grilled between two slices of rye bread. I was raised in a kosher home, which meant eating meat and milk together was prohibited. Couple that with the fact that I never really enjoyed the taste of corned beef, and you can understand why I never bothered to try a Reuben. After going vegan, I tried the tempeh Reuben at Caravan of Dreams, a favorite vegan restaurant in the East Village, and a love affair began. After many years of playing with this recipe, I present you with my favorite tempeh Reuben.*

TEMPEH REUBEN

Serves 1

1 tablespoon ketchup
1 tablespoon nondairy mayonnaise
2 slices rye bread, lightly toasted
1 slice nondairy Swiss cheese
4 strips tempeh bacon
2 slices beefsteak tomato
1/2 large ripe Hass avocado, cut into 1/8-inch thick slices
3 tablespoons sauerkraut, or to taste

1. In a small bowl, combine the ketchup and mayonnaise, stirring to blend well. Spread the mixture on one side of 1 of the bread slices. Place the cheese slice on the other slice of toasted bread and allow it to melt. Set aside.

2. Sear the tempeh strips in a nonstick medium skillet over medium-high heat for 2 minutes on each side, and then remove them from the pan.

3. Place the tempeh on top of the bread with the dressing. Add the tomato slices on top of the tempeh. Top the tomato with the avocado and sauerkraut. Top the loaded slice of bread with the cheesy slice of bread, cut in half, and serve.

Note: If you prefer a grilled Reuben, do not toast the bread. Instead, lightly butter one side of each bread slice before assembling the sandwich and proceed with the recipe. Once the sandwich is assembled, grill it in a skillet or grill pan, butter-side down, until nicely browned on top.

Variation: To make a Classic Grilled Tempeh Reuben, spread nondairy butter on one side of each slice of bread. Double the amount of ketchup-mayonnaise dressing and spread it on the non-buttered sides of both slices of bread. Omit the avocado and tomato. Double the amount of tempeh bacon and cheese. To assemble the sandwich, place the tempeh bacon on top of the dressing, top the bacon with the sauerkraut, top the sauerkraut with 2 slices nondairy cheese, then top with the remaining slice of bread. Place the sandwich on a hot nonstick skillet or griddle, and cook until the bread is browned and the cheese is melted, turning once to brown the other side.

No visit to New York City is complete without stopping at Yonah Schimmel's Knish Bakery on Manhattan's Lower East Side, where they have been selling knishes since 1890. And they even have vegan ones! At one time, knisheries could be found all over the City, from Coney Island in Brooklyn to Forest Hills in Queens. Even though they never made it as big as bagels, knishes are a quintessential New York food, and we consider them iconic. Try yours with a "schmear" of brown mustard for the truly authentic New York City knish experience. And FYI, the "k" in "knish" is not silent.

KNISHES

Makes 8 to 12 knishes

Dough:
1/2 cup canola oil or other neutral oil
1 teaspoon distilled white vinegar
3/4 cup water
2 1/2 cups unbleached all-purpose flour
1 teaspoon baking powder
1/2 teaspoon salt

Filling:
3 medium Yukon gold potatoes, peeled and quartered
1 tablespoon olive oil
1 small onion, cut into 1/4-inch pieces
1 tablespoon nondairy butter
1/2 teaspoon salt
Ground black pepper, to taste
Plain unsweetened nondairy milk, for brushing

1. In a small bowl combine the canola oil, vinegar, and water. Mix well.

2. In a large bowl, whisk together the flour, baking powder, and salt. Make a well in the center of the flour mixture and pour in the oil mixture. Mix until just combined, then knead lightly into a ball for 1 minute (the dough will feel somewhat oily). Cover the bowl with plastic wrap and let the dough sit for 1 hour at room temperature to relax. While the dough is relaxing, prepare the filling.

3. Fill a large pot with water. Add the potatoes and bring them to a boil over high heat. Reduce the heat to medium and cook until the potatoes are fork-tender, about 20 minutes. Drain and transfer the potatoes to a large bowl to cool.

4. While the potatoes are cooling, heat the olive oil in a small skillet over medium heat. Add the onion and cook, stirring frequently, until nicely caramelized, about 25 minutes. Add the onion, butter, salt, and pepper to the potatoes and mash them together. The mixture should be smooth with no big lumps. Now it is time to make the knishes.

5. Preheat the oven to 350°F. Line 2 (18 x 12-inch) baking sheets with parchment paper and set aside. Divide the dough in half. On a floured work surface, roll one of the dough halves as thin as you can into a rectangle without tearing it.

6. Use the mashed potatoes to create a 2-inch thick log across the bottom of one of the long sides

of the rectangle. Carefully roll the dough once to wrap the dough around the filling log. Make two additional rolls so you end up with three layers of dough wrapped around the potato filling. Don't roll it too tightly or else it will break open while cooking.

7. To shape the knish, pinch the log of potato-filled dough off at 2- or 3-inch lengths, give it a twist and then cut it off. Pinch the ends shut to enclose the filling. Place the knish upright on the work surface and press it down with your hand to form a squat, round shape. Press the cut side down with your hand to keep it from puffing up in the oven.

8. Repeat these steps until all the dough and filling are used up. You can now bake the knishes, refrigerate them for a few days, or freeze them for up to 3 months.

9. To bake the knishes, place them on the prepared baking sheets, brush them with a little milk and cook them for 30 to 40 minutes, or until the crust is golden. If preparing frozen knishes, let them thaw and then bake as directed. Serve warm.

The Egyptian Gift

Falafel is ubiquitous throughout Middle Eastern cultures. Believed to have originated in Egypt, where it was made with fava beans, falafel migrated north to the Levant, where chickpeas became the bean of choice. In all Middle Eastern cultures, these fried croquettes are nearly always served with pita or laffa, tahini, and fresh vegetables, such as tomatoes, lettuce, and cucumbers. In New York City, there is no shortage of falafel and the seasonings vary with the diversity of the immigrant communities from which they come. Israeli falafel tends to be heavier on the parsley, whereas Palestinian and Lebanese falafel has more cumin, cilantro, and coriander. Egyptians still make theirs with fava beans, and this can be found in many of the Egyptian restaurants around the New York City metropolitan area, which is home to the largest population of Egyptians in the United States.

Food carts selling falafel can be found all over Manhattan. Once a week, the Taïm falafel truck is parked near our office on lower 5th Avenue in Flatiron, and we will often treat ourselves to a sandwich for lunch. We make our falafel Israeli-style, like Taïm's, with a lot of fresh parsley. These delicious balls of fried ground chickpeas are perfect in a pita with Hummus (page 75), Spiced Carrots (page 139), and Israeli Salad (page 128). You can also add them to a salad or simply eat them on their own.

FALAFEL

Makes 30 falafel

2 1/2 cups dried chickpeas, soaked in water for 14 hours
1 cup finely chopped fresh parsley
1/2 small onion, coarsely chopped
4 cloves garlic, finely chopped
1 teaspoon paprika
Salt and ground black pepper, to taste
1 tablespoon sesame seeds
2 tablespoons dry breadcrumbs
1 tablespoon baking soda
Canola oil or other neutral oil, for frying

1. Drain and rinse the chickpeas, then transfer them to a food processor. Add the parsley, onion, garlic, paprika, and salt and pepper. Process this mixture to make a coarse, damp paste. Add a little water if the mixture is too dry.

2. Transfer the mixture to a medium mixing bowl. Add the sesame seeds and breadcrumbs. Mix well. Cover and refrigerate for 30 minutes to 1 hour.

3. Remove the mixture from the refrigerator, add the baking soda and mix well. Shape the mixture into walnut-size balls.

4. Heat 4 inches of oil in a large pot over high heat. Carefully add a few falafel balls to the oil. Do not overcrowd the pot. Fry until the balls are golden brown, about 5 minutes. Remove the balls from the oil with a slotted spoon and transfer them to a paper towel–lined plate to absorb any excess oil. Repeat this process until all the falafel are fried.

Note: If the falafel are browning too quickly, lower the heat. You want to be sure they are cooked completely through, not burnt on the outside and raw in the middle.

Many of the once ubiquitous hot dog carts in New York City have been edged out by The Halal Guys. This chain offers Middle Eastern fare, such as falafel and gyros, but one of the most popular items on their menu is the combination platter. This plate consists of assorted grilled meats topped with shredded iceberg lettuce, diced tomatoes, and a generous coating of "white sauce." We re-created this signature dish with seitan, Soy Curls, and a vegan white sauce. If you want to make this gluten-free, use Beefy Soy Curls (page 13) in place of the seitan.

STREET MEAT PLATTER

Serves 8 to 10

Beefy Seitan:
1 tablespoon plain unsweetened nondairy yogurt
2 shallots, minced
2 cloves garlic, minced
2 teaspoons grated fresh ginger
1 1/4 teaspoons salt
1 teaspoon cornstarch
1/2 teaspoon ground cumin
1 teaspoon ground coriander
1/2 teaspoon curry powder
1/2 teaspoon ground cinnamon
1/2 teaspoon paprika
1/4 teaspoon ground allspice
1/4 teaspoon ground black pepper
1 pound Beefy Seitan (page 11) or store-bought seitan, finely chopped

Chicken-Style Soy Curls:
2 tablespoons plain unsweetened nondairy yogurt
1 clove garlic, grated
1 teaspoon grated fresh ginger
1 teaspoon salt
1 teaspoon ground coriander
1/2 teaspoon curry powder
1/4 teaspoon ground cumin
1/4 teaspoon ground black pepper
1/4 teaspoon ground turmeric
Pinch ground white pepper
6 cups Chicken-Style Soy Curls (page 14), coarsely chopped
5 tablespoons extra-virgin olive oil, divided
Steamed rice, shredded iceberg lettuce, and diced tomatoes, for serving
White Sauce (page 66), for serving

1. **Beefy Seitan:** In a large bowl, combine the yogurt, shallots, garlic, ginger, salt, cornstarch, cumin, coriander, curry powder, cinnamon, paprika, allspice, and pepper. Mix well. Add the seitan and toss to thoroughly coat. Cover the bowl and refrigerate at least 1 hour, preferably overnight.

2. **Chicken-Style Soy Curls:** In a large bowl, combine the yogurt, garlic, ginger, salt, coriander, curry powder, cumin, black pepper, turmeric, and white pepper and mix well. Add the Soy Curls and toss to coat. Cover and refrigerate at least 1 hour, preferably overnight.

3. Heat 2 tablespoons of the oil in a large nonstick skillet over medium-high heat. Add the marinated chicken-style Soy Curls and sauté until lightly browned, about 8 minutes. Transfer the Soy Curls to a plate.

4. Heat another 2 tablespoons of the oil in the same skillet over medium-high heat. Add the marinated seitan and press it down into a giant patty, but do not break it up. Cook the seitan until nicely browned on one side, about 3 minutes. Flip and cook 4 minutes on the other side. It is okay if it doesn't stay in one piece. Once the patty is browned on both sides, remove it from the skillet and transfer it to a plate.

5. Heat the remaining 1 tablespoon oil in the same skillet over medium-high heat. Return the Soy Curls and the seitan to the skillet and cook, breaking up the seitan into smaller chunks. Cook for 1 minute and season with salt and pepper to taste. Serve the seitan and soy curl mixture over steamed rice with a handful of iceberg lettuce and tomato. Pour a generous amount of the white sauce over the top.

WHITE SAUCE

Makes 1 1/2 cups

When you say "white sauce" to a non-New Yorker, they will likely think of an Alfredo sauce or other cream sauce to go over pasta. To a New Yorker, however, white sauce is the magical dressing used by the Halal Guys at their food carts all over the city. For years, people have tried to find out exactly what is in the sauce, but they will not share their secret recipe. This sauce is perfect for drizzling on top of our Street Meat Combo Platter (page 65), on our Southern-Fried Seitan (page 107) or even as a condiment for French Fries (page 143). It also works great on roasted vegetables, grilled seitan, or even as sandwich spread in place of vegan mayonnaise.

- 1 1/2 cups plain unsweetened nondairy yogurt
- 2 tablespoons tahini
- 1 clove garlic, minced
- 2 tablespoons water
- 1 teaspoon salt
- 1/4 teaspoon ground black pepper

Combine the yogurt, tahini, garlic, water, salt, and pepper in a small bowl. Mix well. Cover and refrigerate for at least 1 hour. Bring to room temperature before using.

Our Street Food Carts

The story of food being sold from street carts in New York is as old as the City itself. Immigrants to the Dutch port of New Amsterdam frequently took jobs as food vendors, selling the foods from their home countries on city streets. Interestingly, oysters and clams were the first street cart foods sold in New York City. As immigrants continued to come to the City, the menus changed, reflecting the tastes of each new arriving culture. However, one food has been a constant in the pushcart trade since the early nineteenth century: the soft pretzel. In the early 1800s, German immigrants introduced the soft pretzel to the people of New York. Since then, soft pretzels have remained a New York City street food staple. Soft pretzels are so synonymous with New York City's street food culture, they even inspired an episode of Seinfeld, arguably one of the most quintessential New York television shows. The "These Pretzels Are Making Me Thirsty" bit continues to live on long after the series ended.

The soft pretzel has been sold on the streets of New York City since at least the 1820s. Today, they are sold from ubiquitous metal carts found all over Manhattan and always offered with mustard. Unfortunately, those pretzels aren't vegan—but don't worry, we gotcha covered.

STREET CART PRETZELS

Makes 8

1 1/2 cups warm water (110°F to 115°F)
1 tablespoon sugar
2 teaspoons kosher salt
1 (1/4-ounce) package active dry yeast
4 1/2 cups unbleached all-purpose flour
2 tablespoons nondairy butter, melted
Canola oil or other neutral oil, as needed
10 cups water
2/3 cup baking soda
Coarse salt, as needed

1. Combine the warm water, sugar, and kosher salt in the bowl of a stand mixer and sprinkle the yeast on top. Allow this mixture to sit for 5 minutes or until it begins to foam. Add the flour and butter. Using the dough hook attachment, mix the ingredients on low speed until well combined. Increase the speed to medium and knead until the dough is smooth and pulls away from the side of the bowl, 4 to 5 minutes.

2. Remove the dough from the bowl, clean the bowl, and grease it well with oil. Return the dough to the bowl, cover it with plastic wrap, and let it sit in a warm place for 50 to 55 minutes, or until the dough has doubled in size.

3. Preheat the oven to 450°F. Line 2 (18 x 12-inch) baking pans with parchment paper and lightly brush with oil. Set the pans aside.

4. Bring the water and the baking soda to a rolling boil in an 8-quart pot over high heat. While waiting for the water to boil, shape the pretzels. Transfer the dough to a lightly oiled work surface and divide it into 8 equal pieces. Roll out each piece of dough into a 24-inch rope. Make a "U" shape with the rope. Holding the ends of the rope, cross them over each other and press them on to the bottom of the "U" in order to form the shape of a pretzel. Place the pretzels on the prepared baking sheets.

5. One at a time, place the pretzels into the boiling water for 30 seconds. Remove them from the water using a large, flat spatula, return them to the baking sheets, and sprinkle them with the coarse salt. Bake the pretzels until they are light golden brown in color, 12 to 14 minutes. Transfer them to a cooling rack for at least 5 minutes before serving.

Five
START SPREADING THE NEWS

Most New York City apartments are too small to host formal dinners, so it is not uncommon to have friends over for drinks before heading out to dinner. The spreads and dips in this chapter are great for just such an occasion. Serve them with chips for dipping, some olives, and sliced bread for a great meze platter. The sauces here are great staples to keep in the refrigerator to add a little something extra to ordinary meals. Keep a supply of these on hand and your friends will be impressed with how quickly you can pull together a delicious meal. These recipes can stand on their own or be used to complement other recipes in this book.

Michael: *You cannot attend a gathering at my parents' home without my mother serving a store-bought sun-dried tomato basil spread. The first time I brought our vegan version to their home, not only did everyone love it, but they actually preferred it to the store-bought, nonvegan version. This versatile spread is not only great as an appetizer with crackers but it's also wonderful when stirred into hot pasta to make a creamy sauce.*

SUN-DRIED TOMATO BASIL SPREAD

Makes 1 1/2 cups

1/2 cup sun-dried tomatoes (not oil-packed), coarsely chopped
8 ounces nondairy cream cheese, softened
4 tablespoons nondairy butter, softened
1 clove garlic, coarsely chopped
2 tablespoons tomato paste
1/4 cup fresh basil, coarsely chopped
1 tablespoon dried basil

1. Place the sun-dried tomatoes in a heat-proof bowl and cover them with hot water. Set aside for 10 minutes. Drain the tomatoes and pat dry.

2. In a food processor, combine the tomatoes, cream cheese, butter, garlic, tomato paste, fresh basil, and dried basil. Process until completely smooth, about 2 minutes. Transfer the mixture to a bowl, cover, and refrigerate for at least 1 hour.

3. Before serving, allow the spread to sit out for about 10 minutes to soften a little. Store leftovers, covered, in the refrigerator for up to 1 week.

Having a garden is not possible for most New Yorkers. While some people do grow fresh herbs in small pots on their windowsills, this is unfortunately not an option for most people. This herb spread uses dried herbs, but tastes like you used freshly picked ones from your garden. If you want to make this with fresh herbs, you will need three times more than the amounts of dried herbs called for in the recipe. Serve this spread with crackers as an hors d'oeuvre or use it on sandwiches.

GARDEN HERB SPREAD

Makes 1 1/2 cups

2 garlic cloves, minced
4 tablespoons nondairy butter, softened
8 ounces nondairy cream cheese, at room temperature
1 tablespoon nutritional yeast
1/2 teaspoon dried dill weed
1 teaspoon dried marjoram
1 teaspoon dried basil
1 teaspoon dried chives
1/4 teaspoon ground black pepper
1/4 teaspoon dried thyme
1 tablespoon fresh parsley, minced

1. In a food processor, combine the garlic, butter, cream cheese, and nutritional yeast and pulse to combine. Add the dill weed, marjoram, basil, chives, pepper, thyme, and parsley. Process for 2 minutes to thoroughly combine. Transfer the mixture to a small bowl, cover, and refrigerate for at least 1 hour.

2. Bring the spread to room temperature before serving. Store any leftovers, covered, in the refrigerator for up to 1 week.

Farming in Manhattan

New York City is not typically thought of as an agricultural center. However, there are over seven hundred food-producing urban farms and gardens citywide. Throughout the City, vacant lots, rooftops, schoolyards, and New York City Housing Authority gardens are being transformed into places to grow food. These gardens do much more than simply provide New Yorkers with fresh produce. They allow gardeners to earn income by selling their crops at farmers' markets, learn about nutrition and the environment, and gain leadership and job skills. There is also a huge benefit to the City in the form of a reduction in garbage, thanks to composting. Many abandoned areas are also being converted into public parks. The most recent addition to the list of public parks in New York City is the High Line. At 1.45 miles long, the High Line park runs from 14th Street to 34th Street on a repurposed abandoned railway track on the west side of Manhattan. The High Line provides visitors with aerial views of both the City and the Hudson River.

Once regarded only as an appetizer at cocktail parties, hummus is finally getting the credit it deserves as a featured item on menus all over the City. Sure, you can buy this at any bodega or supermarket, but home-made tastes so much better.

HUMMUS

Makes 5 cups

1 1/4 cups dried chickpeas
1/2 teaspoon baking soda
2 cups water, plus more for soaking the chickpeas
3 tablespoons tahini
1 clove garlic, minced
4 tablespoons fresh lemon juice
1 teaspoon salt
2 tablespoons extra-virgin olive oil

1. Place the chickpeas in a large mixing bowl. Add the baking soda and cover with 1 inch of water. Allow the chickpeas to soak for 12 hours. After 12 hours, drain the water, add fresh water to the bowl, and soak for 12 more hours.

2. After 24 hours, drain the chickpeas and transfer them to a medium pot. Add 2 cups of water to the chickpeas and bring them to a boil, skimming off any foam. Reduce the heat and simmer for 3 1/2 hours. Drain the chickpeas and reserve the cooking liquid.

3. Transfer the chickpeas to a food processor. Add the tahini, garlic, lemon juice, salt, and olive oil. Process for 5 minutes, stopping to scrape down the side as needed, until the mixture forms a smooth paste. With the processor running, slowly add up to 1 cup of the reserved cooking liquid until you get the desired thickness. Store leftovers in a covered container in the refrigerator for up to 1 week.

When we returned from a trip to Greece, we began seeking out Greek restaurants all over New York City to satisfy our hunger for tzatziki, that delicious combination of yogurt, cucumber, garlic, and lemon. Our search landed us in Astoria, Queens, the heartland for Greek Americans in New York City. Our vegan version of this Greek classic brings us back to eating it with warm pita while watching the sunset in Mykonos.

TZATZIKI

Makes 2 cups

1 large cucumber, peeled
3/4 teaspoon salt, divided
1 (14-ounce) container firm silken tofu, drained
3 tablespoons fresh lemon juice, plus more as needed
1 tablespoon distilled white vinegar
1 clove garlic, minced
2 tablespoons extra-virgin olive oil
Ground black pepper, to taste

1. Slice the cucumber in half lengthwise and scrape out the seeds. Shred the cucumber using the large holes on a box grater or food processor fitted with a shredding blade. Place the shredded cucumber in a colander, sprinkle it with 1/4 teaspoon of the salt, and allow it to drain.

2. In a food processor, combine the tofu, lemon juice, vinegar, and the remaining 1/2 teaspoon salt. Process until smooth. Add the garlic and oil and process again to combine. Season with the black pepper to taste. Add more salt or lemon juice if needed. Transfer to a medium mixing bowl.

3. Squeeze as much water out of the cucumber as you can, working in small batches to make it more effective. You want the cucumber as dry as you can get. Add the cucumber to the tofu mixture and stir to combine. Cover the bowl and refrigerate for a few hours before serving. Store leftovers, covered, in the refrigerator for up to 1 week.

Little Athens

Astoria, Queens, the epicenter of the Greek American community in New York City, is often referred to as Little Athens. Visiting Astoria is almost like walking down the streets in Athens, as you will often hear nothing but Greek being spoken. Astoria attracts visitors from all over, including Greeks and Greek Americans who want a taste of their home country while in the Big Apple. Although the Greek immigration to New York City did not begin until the late 1960s, by the mid-1970s, Greeks owned almost all of the coffee shops in the City. To this day, no one quite knows how that happened. Even though most of those coffee shops are no longer owned by Greeks today, they all still use the same paper coffee cups with a blue and white Greek key pattern.

Anyone who grew up in the seventies and eighties like we did will tell you that onion dip was a staple at almost any gathering from a swanky cocktail party to a Super Bowl party. One envelope of powered soup mix and sour cream was all you needed to whip up a dip that everyone loved. After lots of work we finally came up the perfect combination of ingredients to match the familiar taste from our childhood. This dip never fails to please, and it's a perfect last-minute recipe. Just break out some chips and veggies and start dipping.

ONION DIP

Makes about 1 1/2 cups

1 vegan beef bouillon cube or 1 teaspoon vegan beef bouillon paste
3 tablespoons dried minced onion
3 tablespoons canned fried onion pieces
1 teaspoon onion powder
1 teaspoon garlic powder
1 1/2 teaspoons soy sauce
1/2 teaspoon balsamic vinegar
1 (12-ounce) container nondairy sour cream

1. Place the bouillon cube in a medium mixing bowl and use a fork to break it up.

2. Add the minced onion, fried onions, onion powder, garlic powder, soy sauce, balsamic vinegar and sour cream to the bowl and mix thoroughly to combine.

3. Serve immediately, or cover and keep in the refrigerator until you need it. If you make this ahead of time, take it out of the refrigerator about 15 minutes before serving, allow to warm up a little bit, and give it a good stir to smooth it out.

Hillstone (formerly Houston's) is a New York City institution. It's an upscale barbecue restaurant that we frequented in our pre-vegan days. Their spinach-artichoke dip is legendary and was, in our opinion, a reason to eat there. When going vegan, this was one of the earlier recipes we veganized. Even though the popular vegan restaurant chain, byCHLOE, now serves a delectable Kale-Artichoke dip, we're still partial to our spinach version.

SPINACH ARTICHOKE DIP

Makes about 3 cups

1 tablespoon extra-virgin olive oil
1 medium onion, cut into 1/4-inch pieces
1 medium clove garlic, minced
4 cups packed fresh spinach leaves, chopped
1 (15-ounce) can cannellini beans, drained and rinsed
2 tablespoons nutritional yeast
2 tablespoons Cashew Parmesan (page 16) or store-bought nondairy Parmesan
1/4 cup water
2 teaspoons tamari
1 teaspoon salt
1 (8-ounce) container nondairy cream cheese, softened
1 (14-ounce) can artichoke hearts, drained, rinsed, and roughly chopped
Salt, to taste
Ground black pepper, to taste
1/4 cup dry breadcrumbs

1. Preheat the oven to 400°F. Lightly oil an 8 x 8-inch baking dish. Set aside.

2. Heat the oil in large skillet over medium heat. Add the onion and sauté until soft and translucent, and just starting to turn golden, about 7 minutes. Add the garlic and sauté for 30 seconds. Add the spinach and sauté until spinach is wilted, 2 to 3 minutes. Remove the pan from the heat.

3. Combine the beans, nutritional yeast, cashew Parmesan, water, tamari, and salt in a food processor and process until completely smooth. Transfer the mixture to a large mixing bowl.

4. Add the cream cheese to the bowl with the bean mixture and mix well to thoroughly combine. Add the artichoke hearts and the spinach mixture and mix well to thoroughly combine. Taste the mixture and add salt and pepper as needed.

5. Spread mixture into the prepared baking dish. Sprinkle the breadcrumbs on top. Cover the dish with foil and bake 20 minutes. After 20 minutes, remove the foil and bake for 10 minutes more until the top is lightly browned.

6. Remove from the oven and allow to cool slightly before serving.

Ethan: *Guac and chips are available at any Mexican restaurant in New York City. Michael thought he didn't like guacamole . . . until he tried mine. Made with onions fried in extra-virgin olive oil, my version was handed down to me by Rosa, my family's housekeeper from Argentina. This quintessentially Italian influence on a timeless Mexican staple is the kind of fusion of cultures that embodies the best of New York City. Serve this deliciousness with your favorite tortilla chips.*

GUACAMOLE

Serves 4

1 tablespoon extra-virgin olive oil
1 large yellow onion, finely chopped
2 ripe Hass avocados
4 tablespoons fresh lime juice
Salt, to taste
Ground black pepper, to taste

1. Heat the oil in a large skillet over medium-high heat. Add the onion and sauté until golden brown, 5 to 6 minutes. Set the onion aside to cool.

2. Cut the avocados in half, remove the pits, and peel them. Put the peeled avocados in a medium mixing bowl. Mash them with a fork, being sure to leave some larger pieces. Add the cooled onions and any remaining oil in the skillet to the bowl with the avocados. Mix well until evenly combined. Add 1 tablespoon of lime juice at a time while sprinkling in small amounts of salt and pepper. Mix well and taste after each addition. Continue to adjust by adding more lime juice, salt, and pepper to taste. This is best served within a few hours of making, or else the avocado will start to turn brown.

This French sauce is derived from a Dutch fish sauce. No wonder the residents of New Amsterdam (a.k.a. New York City) love it so much. Hollandaise sauce transforms a simple piece of tofu on an English muffin into Tofu Benedict (page 34) and makes a great accompaniment to Roasted Asparagus (page 114).

HOLLANDAISE SAUCE

Makes 1 1/2 cups

4 tablespoons nondairy butter
2 tablespoons unbleached all-purpose flour (use rice flour for a gluten-free option)
Pinch ground turmeric
6 tablespoons white wine
3 tablespoons fresh lemon juice
1 1/2 cups plain unsweetened nondairy milk
4 teaspoons nutritional yeast
1/4 teaspoon salt

1. In a small saucepan over medium heat, combine the butter, flour, and turmeric and cook, stirring, for 3 minutes. Whisk in the white wine and cook for 2 minutes. Whisk in the lemon juice and cook until it becomes a thick sauce. Add the milk and whisk until smooth.

2. Reduce the heat to low and simmer for 5 minutes, whisking continuously. Remove the saucepan from the heat and add the nutritional yeast and salt. Whisk well to make sure there are no lumps. Keep warm until ready to use.

In small New York City apartments, the last thing you want to do on a hot summer day is keep your stove on. This means making a slowly simmered homemade tomato sauce is something for colder weather. This quick and easy sauce requires no heat. It is ideal for use in recipes that call for baking or roasting, such as the Classic NYC Pizza (page 96), the Lasagna (page 86), or the Mushroom-Stuffed Zucchini (page 120).

NO-COOK TOMATO SAUCE

Makes 3 cups

2 pounds Roma tomatoes, peeled, or 1 (28-ounce) can whole peeled tomatoes, undrained
1 large clove garlic
10 fresh basil leaves
1 teaspoon dried oregano
1/2 teaspoon salt
1/4 teaspoon ground black pepper

In a food processor, combine the tomatoes and their juice, garlic, basil, oregano, salt, and pepper, and pulse until everything is mixed and there are no chunks of tomato or garlic left. You should have a red sauce with flecks of green from the basil. Taste and adjust the seasonings, if needed. Use the sauce immediately or store, covered, in the refrigerator for up to 1 week.

Six
SUPPER CLUB

New York City is home to some of the finest restaurants in the world. With over twenty-seven thousand restaurants to choose from, many New Yorkers don't use their kitchens for cooking. For them, ovens and cupboards often become extra storage for clothing. Dinner in New York City can be an elaborate formal affair at a five-star restaurant, an intimate candlelit meal overlooking the skyline, a pop-up experience by an up-and-coming chef, or simply getting food delivered from the Chinese place on the corner. Because the City has such a wide variety of ethnicities, deciding what main dishes to choose for this book was a challenge. These are ones that we really enjoy and will give you a taste of dinner in New York City.

Lasagna is the ultimate Italian comfort food, and you can get it everywhere in New York City. Whether you're at a pizza joint, an Italian restaurant, or a diner, this gooey, cheesy, tomato saucy, noodley goodness awaits your mere order. Ethan grew up eating lasagna because his mother would make it on the weekends in order to have leftovers for the coming week. Michael, on the other hand, never ate lasagna until he started making it (at Ethan's request). We use our homemade Tofu Ricotta (page 17) in our lasagna, and it really adds the creamy texture that people expect. Whenever we serve this to nonvegan friends and family, we're always asked the same question: "What kind of cheese is this?" This is the perfect first meal to make for your future-vegan, currently omnivore boyfriend or girlfriend. Really. You just gotta take our word for it. Oh, and invite us to the wedding.

LASAGNA

Serves 8 to 10

1 tablespoon salt
12 lasagna noodles
1 tablespoon extra-virgin olive oil
1 medium onion, cut into 1/4-inch pieces
1 clove garlic, minced
1 pound fresh spinach, washed and undried
3 cups No-Cook Tomato Sauce (page 83) or store-bought marinara sauce
3 1/2 cups Tofu Ricotta (page 17) or store-bought nondairy ricotta
1/2 cup shredded nondairy mozzarella cheese
1/4 cup Cashew Parmesan (page 16) or store-bought nondairy Parmesan

1. Lightly oil an 18 x 12-inch baking sheet and set aside. Bring a large pot of water to a boil. Add the salt and the lasagna noodles. Cook until the noodles are pliable, about 6 minutes. Drain the noodles and arrange them individually on the prepared baking sheet so they don't stick together.

2. Heat the oil in a large skillet over medium heat. Add the onion and sauté for 5 minutes, or until it is soft and translucent. Add the garlic and sauté for 30 more seconds. Add the spinach in batches, one handful at a time. Toss well to incorporate it with the onion and garlic. As it wilts, add more spinach. Continue until all the spinach is wilted. Transfer the spinach mixture to a colander and drain out as much liquid as possible. Use your hands to press out the liquid. You should end up with about one-third the volume you started with. Set aside.

3. Preheat the oven to 400°F. Lightly oil a 9 x 13-inch baking dish. Spread 3/4 cup no-cook tomato sauce on the bottom of the dish. Arrange 3 lasagna noodles, side-by-side, over the sauce. Spread one-third of the tofu ricotta over the noodles. Top the tofu ricotta with one-third of the spinach mixture. Sprinkle 2 tablespoons mozzarella over the spinach. Sprinkle 1 tablespoon of the cashew Parmesan over the mozzarella. Repeat this process 2 more times: sauce, noodles, tofu ricotta, spinach, mozzarella, and cashew Parmesan. End with a layer of noodles. Top the last layer of noodles with the remaining sauce, mozzarella, and Parmesan.

4. Cover the pan with aluminum foil and bake for 35 minutes. Remove the foil and cook 10 more minutes. Remove the lasagna from the oven and let it cool for a few minutes before serving.

We are both children of the eighties. In New York City during the 1980s, diners were everywhere, always packed, and pot pie was a staple of every diner menu. Whether for lunch or dinner, young and old alike loved breaking open the flaky crust to let the gravy ooze out and expose the medley of vegetables and meat within.

CHICK'N POT PIE

Serves 4

2 tablespoons canola oil or other neutral oil
1/2 large yellow onion, cut into 1/4-inch dice
2 cups chopped white button mushrooms
2 cups vegetable broth
3 tablespoons nutritional yeast
1 vegetable bouillon cube
1/2 teaspoon onion powder
1/2 teaspoon garlic powder
1/2 teaspoon salt
3 tablespoons unbleached all-purpose flour
3 cups assorted frozen vegetables (peas, carrots, corn, green beans, and broccoli)
16 ounces Chicken-Style Seitan (page 12) or store-bought seitan, or 2 cups Chicken-Style Soy Curls (page 14), roughly chopped
1 (12 x 12-inch) sheet vegan puff pastry dough, thawed

1. Preheat the oven to 350°F. Spray an 8 x 8-inch or 9 x 9-inch baking dish with nonstick cooking spray. Or, if you want to make individual servings, use 4 (2-cup) ceramic crocks, the kind that you would use for French onion soup.

2. Heat the oil in a large saucepan over medium-high heat. Add the onion and cook, stirring occasionally, until soft, about 7 minutes. Add the mushrooms and cook, stirring, until very tender, another 6 minutes or so. Add the broth, nutritional yeast, bouillon cube, onion powder, garlic powder, and salt. Bring to simmer, stirring frequently.

3. Slowly add the flour, 1 tablespoon at a time, whisking after each addition to thoroughly combine. After all the flour is incorporated, add the mixed vegetables and stir to combine. Stir in the seitan or Soy Curls. Pour the mixture into the prepared baking dish.

4. Roll out the puff pastry dough to remove any fold lines. If making individual servings, cut the pastry dough into quarters. Arrange the pastry dough over the vegetable mixture and trim off any excess. Cut a few slits in the pastry to allow steam to escape. Bake for 30 minutes, or until the crust is golden brown. Allow to cool slightly before serving, as the filling will be hot.

A stew is the perfect culinary representation of New York City. Just as the city is a mixture of cultures and cuisines, the ingredients of a stew come together to make a dish more flavorful than its individual components. This stew is the embodiment of New York City. We combine red beans for some Latin influence, chickpeas for Middle Eastern flair, potatoes for Northern European heartiness, an assortment of spices, red wine, and coffee (pronounced "kaw-FEE") for a hearty meal that will satisfy everyone.

MELTING-POT STEW

Serves 6 to 8

1 tablespoon extra-virgin olive oil
1 large yellow onion, quartered and cut into 1-inch thick slices
8 ounces cremini mushrooms, cut into 1/8-inch thick slices
5 cloves garlic, minced
3 large carrots, peeled and cut into 1/8-inch thick slices
1 cup full-bodied red wine
1 teaspoon dried rosemary, finely chopped
1 teaspoon dried thyme
1 teaspoon paprika
1 teaspoon salt
1/4 teaspoon ground black pepper
3 cups vegetable broth
8 ounces fingerling potatoes, cut into 1-inch cubes
1 1/2 teaspoons instant coffee grounds or 1 teaspoon freshly brewed coffee
1/4 cup chickpea flour or unbleached all-purpose flour
1/2 cup water
2 tablespoons tomato paste
1 1/2 cups cooked or 1 (15-ounce) can red kidney beans , drained and rinsed
1 1/2 cups cooked or 1 (15-ounce) can chickpeas, drained and rinsed
1/2 teaspoon sherry vinegar

1. Heat the oil in a 4-quart pot over medium-high heat. Add the onion and cook until it is translucent, about 6 minutes. Add the mushrooms and sauté until they have reduced by half, about 5 minutes. Add the garlic and sauté for 30 seconds.

2. Add the carrots, red wine, rosemary, thyme, paprika, salt, and pepper. Bring the mixture to a boil, and cook until the liquid volume is reduced by half, about 5 minutes. Add the vegetable broth and boil for 5 minutes. Add the potatoes and reduce the heat to medium-low. Cook until the potatoes are fork-tender, about 10 minutes. Stir in the instant coffee. In a measuring cup, mix together the flour and water until completely smooth and no lumps remain. Slowly stir the flour and water mixture into the pot and mix well. Add the tomato paste and stir to thoroughly combine. Let the stew thicken for a few minutes.

3. Add the kidney beans and chickpeas to the pot and cook for 5 more minutes. Stir in the sherry vinegar. The stew should be thick and smooth. Taste for seasonings and adjust as needed. Ladle the stew into bowls and serve.

Shepherd's pie made its way to New York City via the Irish and English immigrants who helped build the city. Historically, this dish baked leftover meats and vegetables in a pan lined with mashed potatoes and then topped with more mashed potatoes. It's great for a large gathering and will satisfy even the "I don't like vegan food" crowd.

SHEPHERDLESS PIE

Serves 8 to 10

4 medium russet potatoes, peeled and cut into 1-inch cubes
1 tablespoon canola oil or other neutral oil
3 medium carrots, cut into 1/4-inch pieces
3 celery ribs, cut into 1/4-inch pieces
1 small yellow onion, cut into 1/4-inch pieces
2 cups coarsely chopped cremini mushrooms
3 cups cooked lentils
4 cloves garlic, minced
Salt and ground black pepper, to taste
1 tablespoon tomato paste
1 tablespoon unbleached all-purpose flour
1 teaspoon fresh thyme
1/4 teaspoon dried sage
2 cups vegetable broth
1/3 cup red wine
1 cup plain unsweetened nondairy milk, plus more as needed
2 tablespoons nondairy butter

1. Lightly spray a 9 x 13-inch baking dish with cooking spray. Set aside. In a large pot, combine the potatoes with enough water to cover by 1 inch. Heat the potatoes over high heat and bring them to a boil. Reduce the heat to medium and simmer for 15 minutes, or until the potatoes are soft.

2. While the potatoes are cooking, heat the oil in a large skillet over medium-high heat. Add the carrots, celery, and onion. Sauté until the onion is translucent, about 6 minutes. Add the mushrooms and cook until they begin to brown, about 6 minutes. Add the lentils and mix well. Add the garlic and season with salt and pepper. Mix well. Add the tomato paste and stir to combine. Sprinkle in the flour, stirring, then stir in the thyme and sage. Pour in the vegetable broth and red wine. Mix well and simmer for a few minutes to thicken. Remove the skillet from the heat and transfer the mixture into the prepared baking dish.

3. Drain the potatoes and return them to the pot. Place the pot back on the stove over medium heat to dry the potatoes a little. Add the milk and butter, and mash the potatoes until they are completely smooth. Add more milk as needed. Season with salt and pepper to taste.

4. Preheat the broiler. Spread the mashed potatoes over the top of the vegetable mixture. Don't smooth the potatoes out, as the rougher the surface of the pie, the crispier it will get.

5. Lightly spray the potatoes with nonstick cooking spray and place the baking dish under the broiler for 10 minutes, or until the top is crispy. Watch carefully, as it can burn very quickly. Remove the baking dish from the oven and allow it to cool slightly before serving.

"The city seen from the Queensboro Bridge is always the city seen for the first time, in its first wild promise of all the mystery and the beauty in the world."

— F. Scott Fitzgerald, *The Great Gatsby*

Puerto Ricans have been living in New York City since the middle of the nineteenth century, but it was the Great Migration of the 1940s that firmly rooted Puerto Ricans into the core cultural composition of New York City. There are few foods more typical of Puerto Rico than mofongo. Typically made of fried green plantains mashed in a pilón (a wooden mortar and pestle) with broth, chicharrónes (pork cracklings), garlic, and oil, mofongo is also popular in Cuba and the Dominican Republic. This mofongo uses seasoned seitan to deliver the expected textures and flavors of this quintessential Puerto Rican dish. Serve mofongo on top of cooked rice or with grilled vegetables.

MOFONGO

Serves 4 to 6

4 large whole green plantains

4 cups cold water

1 teaspoon salt

5 tablespoons extra-virgin olive oil, divided

1 teaspoon Adobo Spice Mix (page 94)

1 tablespoon paprika

1/4 teaspoon smoked paprika

8 ounces Basic Seitan (page 9) or store-bought seitan, cut into 1/2-inch pieces

2 cloves garlic, minced

2 tablespoons vegetable broth

1. Peel the plantains and cut them into 1/2-inch slices. In a large bowl, combine the plantain slices, water, and salt. Allow the plantains to soak for 15 minutes. Remove the plantains and transfer them to a plate lined with paper towels to absorb the excess water. While the plantains are soaking, combine 2 tablespoons of the oil, adobo spice mix, paprika, and smoked paprika in a bowl. Add the seitan and toss to coat. Set aside.

2. In a large skillet over medium heat, heat another 2 tablespoons of the oil. Add the plantains to the skillet and fry until they are golden brown, about 3 minutes per side. Remove the plantains and transfer to plate covered with a paper towel to absorb the oil.

3. In the same skillet, add the seitan and cook until it is crispy on all sides, about 5 minutes.

4. Combine the seitan, plantains, garlic, the remaining 1 tablespoon oil, and vegetable broth in a food processor. Pulse until combined into a mashed texture. Don't overprocess; it should be chunky.

5. Fill a 1-cup bowl with one-quarter of the mofongo and press it down to pack it tightly. Loosen the mofongo with a knife around the sides of the bowl, turn it upside down, and drop it on a plate in a mound.

Tip: Plantains look like bananas, but they don't peel as easily. Use a sharp knife to slice the peel lengthwise all around the plantain. Then slice off the top and bottom to make peeling them easier.

Gluten-Free Option: Use Soy Curls in place of seitan. To use Soy Curls, pour 2 cups of boiling water into a large bowl. Dissolve 1 teaspoon vegetable bouillon paste and 1 teaspoon adobo spice mix in the water. Add 1 cup Soy Curls to the bowl and set aside for 10 minutes. After 10 minutes, drain the Soy Curls and squeeze out as much liquid as possible. Roughly chop the Soy Curls and use in place of the seitan.

ADOBO SPICE MIX

Makes about 1/2 cup

You can buy a jar of prepared adobo seasoning, but you probably already have the ingredients on your spice rack. We don't like buying spice blends when we can easily make them. Our adobo spice mix takes just seconds to make.

- 2 tablespoons salt
- 2 tablespoons garlic powder
- 1 tablespoon dried oregano
- 1 teaspoon ground black pepper
- 1 teaspoon ground turmeric
- 1 teaspoon onion powder

Combine all the ingredients in a small bowl. Mix well to make sure all the spices are well distributed. For the mofongo, you only need 1 teaspoon of this mixture. Store the rest in an airtight container for future use.

La Isla del Encanto

Puerto Ricans first immigrated to New York City in the mid-nineteenth century. After the Spanish-American War in 1898, Puerto Ricans were no longer subjects of the Spanish Crown. Though initially considered Puerto Rican citizens of American possession, they were quickly given US citizenship (with limitations) in 1917, allowing them to migrate to New York City. When air travel became more commercialized in the 1950s, the Great Migration began. Puerto Ricans were the first large group of Hispanics to move to New York City. They settled in the Bronx, Brooklyn, and East Harlem (which eventually became known as Spanish Harlem). Today, nearly one in ten New Yorkers is Puerto Rican. Of the City's Hispanic population, one-third is Puerto Rican.

Michael: *Michael: During the year and a half when Ethan was vegan and I was not, there were many vegan restaurants in the city that Ethan enjoyed but I didn't. Having not yet gone vegan, certain foods tasted unfamiliar and different than I expected. When we first went to Blossom, I was thrilled to see seitan piccata on the menu, as the non-vegan version of this dish was one of my favorite meals. Similarly, when we went to Candle 79 for the first time, and I was still not vegan, I was relieved to see seitan piccata as one of its signature dishes. Dining out, for us, became much easier, knowing that there were great vegan restaurants that had dishes on the menu that I would love. One evening, I realized that I could make it at home, and I whipped up this version, which worked on the very first attempt. This recipe is great for a dinner party, because you can do all the cooking early in the day and toss it all together at the last minute before serving.*

SEITAN PICCATA

Serves 4

1/2 cup unbleached all-purpose flour
2 tablespoons paprika
1 teaspoon salt
1/4 teaspoon ground black pepper
16 ounces Chicken-Style Seitan (page 12) or store-bought seitan, sliced into 1/4-inch thick cutlets
4 tablespoons extra-virgin olive oil, divided
8 ounces cremini mushrooms, cut into 1/8-inch thick slices
1 clove garlic, smashed
1 cup white wine
2 tablespoons fresh lemon juice, divided
Canola oil or other neutral oil or olive oil, for frying

1. On a large plate, combine the flour, paprika, salt, and pepper. Dredge each seitan cutlet in the flour mixture, coating each side. Shake off any excess flour.

2. Heat 2 tablespoons of the olive oil in a large skillet over medium-high heat. Add the seitan cutlets to the skillet and cook for 2 minutes, or until lightly browned. Flip the cutlets over and cook on the other side for 2 more minutes. Transfer the seitan to a paper towel–lined plate to drain.

3. Heat the remaining 2 tablespoons olive oil in the same skillet. Add the mushrooms and garlic and sauté until the volume of mushrooms is about half the volume you started with, about 10 minutes. Remove and discard the garlic. Pour the white wine into the skillet and let it boil for 1 minute. Scrape up any browned bits from the bottom of the skillet, then reduce the heat to medium. Add 1 tablespoon of the lemon juice to the pan. Taste the sauce and add a little salt if needed. If you want a stronger lemon flavor, add the remaining 1 tablespoon lemon juice.

4. Note: If you are making this ahead of time, stop here. Remove the sauce from the heat and cover. When you are ready to serve, reheat the sauce and continue.

5. Return the seitan cutlets to the skillet and stir to coat the cutlets in the sauce. Cook the seitan in the sauce for 5 minutes. Serve hot.

Tip: Remember this important rule for cooking with wine: if you wouldn't drink it, don't cook with it! Also, if the wine you use is very acidic, you should go lighter on the lemon juice. You want to stick to a more full-bodied white wine and avoid the lighter ones.

Nothing says New York City like a slice of pizza. No matter where you are in the City, you are never more than a few minutes away from a fresh, hot slice. Whether it's John's, Joe's, or some other place, everyone has a favorite pizza joint. A visit to New York City simply isn't complete without having pizza.

CLASSIC NYC PIZZA

Serves 4

Unbleached all-purpose flour, for dusting
1 pound Pizza Dough (page 8) or store-bought pizza dough, at room temperature
Extra-virgin olive oil, as needed
Garlic powder, to taste
Salt, to taste
Dried oregano, to taste
3/4 cup No-Cook Tomato Sauce (page 83) or store-bought marinara sauce
1/2 cup shredded nondairy mozzarella cheese
Red pepper flakes, optional, for serving
Cashew Parmesan (page 16) or store-bought nondairy Parmesan, for serving

1. If you are using a pizza stone, place the pizza stone in the oven and preheat it to 500°F. (A really hot oven and stone are key to getting a crispy crust.) If you are not using a stone, simply preheat the oven. If you are using a pizza stone, flour a piece of parchment paper or wooden cutting board and stretch the dough to the size of your stone on the paper or board. If you are using a pizza pan, lightly dust a work surface with flour.

2. Stretch the dough to the size of your pizza pan and place it on the pan. Lightly brush the dough with the oil. Season it with the garlic powder, salt, and oregano. Spoon the no-cook tomato sauce in the center of the dough. Starting in the center of the sauce, use a large spoon to spread the sauce in a circle over the dough, leaving a 3/4-inch border all the way around. Sprinkle the sauce with a little more dried oregano and salt. Top the pizza with the mozzarella cheese and whatever other toppings you like.

3. If you are using a stone, carefully slide the dough from the parchment or board onto the stone. If you are using a pan, put the pan in the oven. Bake the pizza for 10 minutes or until the edges are slightly golden and the cheese is melted. Remove the pizza from the oven and let it cool slightly before slicing. Serve the pizza with the red pepper flakes (if using), cashew Parmesan, and additional garlic powder.

Ethan: *Freshly grated ginger is what makes this recipe really pop. When I lived in Tokyo for a year before med school, I fell in love with fresh ginger and learned to use it in nearly everything I cooked. In our pre-vegan days, when we would eat out in Chinatown, we gravitated toward crispy fried dishes served in a sticky, sweet sauce. When we went vegan, we re-created that type of dish first with seitan and later with Soy Curls. Both versions are way better than anything we ever ate in Chinatown. Though you can prep this in the morning and cook it up that evening, it tastes best when the vegan meat has had the chance to marinate overnight. Michael and I love to serve this with some steamed rice and broccoli for the quintessential NYC Chinese food experience.*

CRISPY GINGER SEITAN

Serves 4

1 pound Beefy Seitan (page 11) or store-bought seitan, sliced into 1/4-inch thick strips, or Beefy Soy Curls (page 13)

Marinade:
1 tablespoon fresh lemon juice
2 tablespoons soy sauce
1 tablespoon dry white wine or sherry
1 teaspoon sugar
2 tablespoons grated fresh ginger
3 tablespoons canola oil or other neutral oil

Coating:
1/2 cup unbleached all-purpose flour
1 tablespoon cornstarch
2 teaspoons sugar

Sauce:
2 tablespoons water
1 tablespoon cornstarch
2 tablespoons dry white wine or sherry
1/4 cup soy sauce
2 tablespoons rice vinegar
6 tablespoons agave nectar
1 teaspoon sesame oil
2 tablespoons fresh lemon juice

1. In a medium bowl, combine the lemon juice, soy sauce, white wine, sugar, and ginger and stir to fully combine. Add the seitan to the marinade, cover, and set aside for at least 1 hour (but preferably overnight). The longer it sits, the better it will taste.

2. Heat the canola oil in a large skillet over medium-high heat. Preheat the oven to 200°F. While the oil is heating, add the flour, cornstarch, and sugar to a sealable plastic bag and shake the bag to mix the coating.

3. Remove the seitan from the marinade and blot it dry with paper towels. If you are using Soy Curls, squeeze out as much excess liquid as possible. Add the seitan strips to the bag with the coating and shake to coat all the strips.

4. Add the seitan strips to the skillet and sauté until they are browned and crispy, about 5 minutes. Remove the seitan strips from the oil with a slotted spoon and transfer them to a paper towel–lined plate to drain. Keep the seitan warm in the oven until ready to serve.

5. In a small bowl, mix the water and cornstarch and set aside.

6. In a small saucepan, combine the white wine, soy sauce, rice vinegar, agave nectar, sesame oil, and lemon juice. Bring to a boil and then reduce the heat to a simmer. Add the cornstarch mixture to the sauce and stir until the sauce thickens. Pour the sauce over the seitan strips and toss to coat the strips evenly. Serve immediately.

Tip: If you want to make this gluten-free, use Soy Curls, gluten-free soy sauce, and rice flour.

"No place epitomizes the American experience and the American spirit more than New York City."

— Michael R. Bloomberg

Michael: *When I was growing up, there was one smell that always said home to me: my mom's brisket. Brisket is the quintessential food for New York Jews on the High Holidays, and everyone insists their mother or grandmother makes the best one. When I went vegan, I was determined to figure out a way to enjoy a vegan version of this classic. After all, a good brisket is really all about the gravy. My mom's secret ingredient, which I am sharing here at serious risk to my life, is instant coffee.*

BRISKET OF SEITAN

Serves 8 to 10

4 tablespoons canola oil or other neutral oil, divided
3 pounds Beefy Seitan (page 11) or store-bought seitan
2 large onions, sliced into 1/8-inch thick rings
2 tablespoons paprika
2 cups tomato juice, divided, plus more as needed
2 cups water, plus more as needed
2 large carrots, peeled and cut into 1/8-inch thick slices
2 large celery ribs, cut into 1/4-inch thick slices
1 rounded teaspoon vegan beef bouillon paste or 1 vegan beef bouillon cube
1 dried bay leaf
1 1/2 teaspoons instant coffee grounds or 1 teaspoon freshly brewed coffee

1. Heat 2 tablespoons of the oil in a large skillet over medium-high heat. Add the seitan and sear on one side, about 3 minutes. Flip the seitan and sear on the other side, about 2 minutes. Remove the seitan from the skillet and transfer it to a plate.

2. Heat the remaining 2 tablespoons oil in the same skillet. Add the onions and coat them with the paprika. Sauté the onions until deeply browned and reduced in volume by three-quarters, about 8 minutes. It is okay if some of the paprika sticks to the bottom of the skillet. When the onions are dark, but not burnt, reduce the heat to medium. Add 1 cup of the tomato juice to the skillet and use a metal spatula or wooden spoon to scrape up any bits that stuck to the bottom.

3. Once the pan is deglazed, add the remaining 1 cup of tomato juice and the water. Stir well. Add the carrots and celery to the skillet. Raise the heat to bring the mixture to a boil. Cook for 8 minutes, continually scraping the bottom of the skillet. Add the bouillon paste and bay leaf and mix well. Add the seitan back to the skillet. Reduce the heat to just below a simmer and cover the skillet with its lid slightly ajar (you want some steam to escape). Cook for 30 minutes, stirring occasionally, turning the seitan every 10 minutes. If the sauce becomes too thick, stir in another cup of water and another cup of tomato juice.

4. After 30 minutes, use a slotted spoon to remove the seitan and the vegetables. Set them aside, and keep them warm. Remove and discard the bay leaf. Raise the heat to medium-high and bring the gravy to a boil. Allow the gravy to reduce a little bit. It should be thicker than a broth. Add the instant coffee and stir well. Serve the seitan on a platter surrounded by the cooked vegetables. Pour some of the gravy over the top and serve the rest on the side.

Note: For an authentic Vegan Mos experience, leftover gravy is the perfect dip for potato chips. Don't heat it up; simply enjoy it cold right out of the refrigerator. Ethan resisted this for a while, but when he finally tried it, he understood. I've even made the gravy on its own just to have for dipping. Yeah, you laugh now—but trust me, you'll be dipping, too.

General Tso's chicken is arguably one of the most famous Chinese dishes to have been invented in the United States. According to menus in Chinese restaurants all across the country, this dish is named after nineteenth century military strategist General Tso Tsung-t'ang. While it is agreed that this dish was actually created in New York City in the early 1970s, there is a dispute over who actually invented it. (See story opposite.) You easily can adjust the heat of this dish to suit your own tastes. To add more heat, simply break open the chiles when you sauté them so the seeds come out. The seeds hold the heat. Leave them whole for a milder dish. You can make this dish with seitan or Soy Curls for a gluten-free option. Serve with steamed rice and broccoli for the full takeout experience.

GENERAL TSO'S CHICK'N

Serves 6

Sauce:
1/4 cup cornstarch
1/4 cup water
2 cloves garlic, minced
1/2 teaspoon grated fresh ginger
3/4 cup sugar
1/2 cup soy sauce
1/4 cup rice vinegar
1/4 cup sherry or dry white wine
2 cups vegetable broth
Canola oil or other neutral oil, for frying

Coating:
1/2 cup cornstarch
1 1/2 pounds Chicken-Style Seitan (page 12) or store-bought seitan, cut into 2-inch pieces, or 6 cups Chicken-Style Soy Curls (page 14)
1 cup thinly sliced green onions
8 small dried red chiles

1. **Sauce:** Combine the cornstarch, water, garlic, ginger, sugar, soy sauce, rice vinegar, sherry, and vegetable broth in a large bowl. Mix until well combined and the sugar is completely dissolved.

2. Heat 3 inches of oil in a large pot over high heat to 350°F. Heat the oven to 200°F. Line an 18 x 12-inch baking sheet with aluminum foil and place a cooling rack or two on the sheet. You will use this to keep the cooked seitan warm until you are ready to toss it with the sauce.

3. **Coating:** Put the cornstarch in a large, sealable, plastic bag. Add the seitan to the bag and shake well to coat. Add the seitan to the hot oil and fry until it is crispy, 2 to 3 minutes. Don't overcrowd the pot as you do not want to lower the temp of the oil by cooking too many pieces at a time. Using a slotted spoon, remove the seitan from the oil and transfer it to a paper towel–lined plate. Repeat this process until all the seitan is fried. Transfer the fried seitan to the prepared cooling rack and put it in the warm oven.

4. Once all the pieces are fried and keeping warm, pour out all but 1 teaspoon oil from the pot and heat it over medium-high heat. Add the green onions and dried chiles and stir-fry about

30 seconds. This is where you can adjust the heat of the sauce to your own taste preferences. If you want a hotter sauce, break open the chiles. Give the sauce mixture a good stir and then carefully pour it into the pot with the onions and chiles. Cook the sauce until it thickens, stirring continually to prevent burning. If the sauce gets too thick, add a little water. It should be thick enough to coat the back of a spoon. Add the seitan to the sauce and heat just until thoroughly heated, about 1 minute.

The Jia-Wang War

The first claim about the origins of General Tso's chicken is that it was created by chef Peng Jia who came to New York in 1973 from Taiwan and began adapting his traditional Hunan recipes to suit American tastes. In 1977, a *New York Times* review called his recipe "a stir-fried masterpiece, sizzling hot both in flavor and temperature." The competing claim about the origins of this dish comes from New York's Shun Lee Palaces. According to Michael Tong, the owner of the Shun Lee Palaces, a Chinese immigrant chef named T. T. Wang invented it at Shun Lee Palace in 1972. Whatever the truth is, we are just happy that someone invented it.

Whether you find yourself in the Russian community in Sheepshead Bay, Little Ukraine in the East Village, or the "Polish Riviera" of Greenpoint, you're bound to find pierogi. These delightful Eastern European dumplings are hearty, satisfying, and can be a meal unto themselves. We make ours old-school, filled with potatoes and caramelized onions and served with a dollop of nondairy sour cream. Because when something this amazing works across so many ethnicities and nationalities, why mess with perfection?

PIEROGI

Makes about 30 pierogi

3 cups unbleached all-purpose flour, plus more for sprinkling and rolling
1 1/2 teaspoons salt, divided
1 cup water, plus more as needed
5 tablespoons canola oil or other neutral oil, divided
2 pounds sweet onions, cut into 1/4-inch pieces
1 1/2 pounds Yukon gold potatoes, peeled and cut into 3/4-inch cubes
3 tablespoons nutritional yeast
3 tablespoons nondairy butter
1/4 teaspoon finely chopped fresh dill weed
1/4 teaspoon ground black pepper
Nondairy sour cream, optional, for serving

1. In a large mixing bowl, combine the flour with 1/2 teaspoon of the salt. Add the water, 2 tablespoons of the oil, and stir until just combined. Place the dough on a lightly floured work surface and knead until it comes together and is just slightly sticky (you don't want it sticking to your hands). Add more flour as needed (up to 1/4 cup) if the dough is too sticky, or more water as needed (up to 1 tablespoon) if the dough is too dry. Lightly flour the ball of dough. Cut it in half and wrap each half in plastic wrap. Refrigerate the dough while you prepare the filling.

2. Heat the remaining 3 tablespoons oil in a medium saucepan over low heat. Add the onions and stir to coat with the oil. Cover, leaving the lid slightly ajar, and cook for 20 minutes, stirring occasionally. After 20 minutes, the onions should be turning slightly golden and getting soft. Sprinkle them with 1/2 teaspoon salt, stir well, and raise the heat to medium. Cook for 10 more minutes, stirring occasionally. The onions should be nicely caramelized. Remove the pan from the heat.

3. While the onions are cooking, prepare the potatoes. In a large pot, cover the potatoes with 1 inch of cold water. Bring the water to a boil and then reduce it to a simmer. Simmer the potatoes for 15 minutes or until easily pierced with a fork. Drain the potatoes and return them to the pot. Return the pot to the stove and heat over low to dry the potatoes a little bit.

4. Using a potato masher, mash the potatoes with the nutritional yeast, butter, dill, the remaining 1/2 teaspoon salt, and pepper, mashing until smooth. Stir in the caramelized onions.

5. When you are ready to make the pierogi, bring a large pot of salted water to a boil while you roll, cut, and fill the pierogi.

6. On a lightly floured work surface, roll out one ball of dough until it is about 1/16-inch thick. Use a 3 1/2-inch or 4-inch round cookie cutter to cut out rounds of dough. Place each one on a

lightly floured baking sheet and cover it with a damp towel while you continue to roll dough and cut out rounds. Repeat this process with the other ball of dough.

7. Place about 1 tablespoon of the filling on one side of each round of dough. Using a finger, dab a little water on the edge of half the circle, fold the other side of dough over the filling, and gently press and slightly pinch the two sides together, sealing the pierogi. Make sure they are completely sealed, so no filling leaks out. Set each pierogi back on the floured baking sheets without overlapping them. If you want to freeze them, put them into a resealable plastic bag in a single layer and top with parchment paper. Add another layer on top, and seal the bag. Freeze until you want to cook them. Frozen pierogi can be put right into boiling water, no need to thaw them first.

8. Boil the pierogi in small batches for 4 minutes. Use a slotted spoon to transfer them to a plate as you prepare the rest. Cover finished ones lightly with aluminum foil to keep warm. Continue until all of the pierogi are boiled. You can serve them now or quickly pan-fry them to give the outside a little crunch. To pan-fry them, right before serving, heat a little butter in a medium skillet over medium heat. Fry pierogi in batches for approximately 2 minutes on each side until golden brown. Drain them on paper towels and serve warm.

Michael: *Before going vegan, I ate a lot of fried chicken. There were times I'd eat it for breakfast, lunch, and dinner all in the same day. Though usually most associated with Southern cuisine, fried chicken can be found in New York City anywhere at any time of the day or night. This recipe makes use of seitan because its texture is similar to chicken. The neutral flavor of seitan puts the seasonings front and center. Because let's face it, more than anything, people want that fried, crunchy, crispy crust with all of its flavor. Well, that and some ketchup.*

SOUTHERN-FRIED SEITAN

Serves 4

1 cup unbleached all-purpose flour
1/4 cup nutritional yeast
1 teaspoon salt
1/4 teaspoon black pepper
1 teaspoon garlic powder
1 teaspoon onion powder
1 teaspoon paprika
1 cup water
1 teaspoon Dijon mustard
2 tablespoons baking powder
2 1/2 cups panko breadcrumbs
1/2 cup vegan barbecue potato chip crumbs
1 cup canola oil or other neutral oil
16 ounces Chicken-Style Seitan (page 12) or store-bought seitan, cut into 2-inch thick strips

1. In a large bowl, combine the flour, nutritional yeast, salt, pepper, garlic powder, onion powder, and paprika.

2. In a medium bowl, mix together the water and mustard. Add half of the flour mixture to the mustard mixture. Mix well to combine. The batter should be completely smooth with no lumps.

3. Add the baking powder, panko, and potato chip crumbs to the remaining flour mixture and mix well.

4. Heat the oil in a large skillet over high heat. Coat the seitan with the flour-mustard mixture, then dredge it in the flour-panko mixture, covering thoroughly. Use your hands to press the coating onto the seitan. Add the seitan to the skillet, and fry until browned on both sides, about 2 minutes per side. Remove the seitan from the skillet and place it on a paper towel–lined plate to drain. Repeat this process until all the seitan is fried. Serve hot.

Ethan: I did my surgical residency at a small community hospital in Gramercy Park. On the rare occasions when I would have time off, I would head down to the East Village to hang out, have a meal, and meet friends. One day, a co-resident introduced me to the famed "Sixth Street" where, between First and Second Avenues, every restaurant on the block is Indian. Being a longtime lover of Indian food, I was so delighted in this discovery that I eventually tried each restaurant on that block. Fast-forward to when Michael and I started dating years later, I discovered that he "didn't like Indian food." As it turns out, he had never tried it! After years of unrelenting persistence, I succeeded in getting him to try it. Early in our relationship, we lived adjacent to Little India. It always tickled me a little when Michael would suggest walking over to one of our favorite spots. Typical of Michael, he tried a few different types of dal and then came up with his own recipe that is probably the best I've ever had.

RED LENTIL DAL

Serves 6 to 8

1 tablespoon canola oil or other neutral oil
1 teaspoon mustard seeds
1 large yellow onion, finely chopped
4 cloves garlic, minced
2 tablespoons finely chopped fresh ginger
1/2 teaspoon cumin seeds
1/4 teaspoon ground cardamom
2 cups red lentils, picked over, rinsed, and drained
4 cups low-sodium vegetable broth
1 1/2 cups chopped tomatoes, fresh or canned, with their juice
1 teaspoon ground turmeric
1 teaspoon fine sea salt

1. In a large skillet, heat the oil over medium-high heat and add the mustard seeds. As soon as the mustard seeds begin to dance a little, about 1 minute, add the onion and cook until it has softened, about 6 minutes. Add the garlic, ginger, cumin seeds, and cardamom. Sauté until fragrant, about 1 minute.

2. Add the lentils, vegetable broth, tomatoes, turmeric, and salt. Bring the dal to a boil, then reduce the heat to medium-low, cover the skillet, and simmer, stirring often, until the lentils are soft, about 15 minutes. Ladle the dal into bowls and serve.

South Asian Specialties

New York City is home to over 315,000 people from the Indian subcontinent. New Yorkers from India, Pakistan, Bangladesh, and Sri Lanka represent nearly 4 percent of the city's population. The greater New York City metropolitan area is home to approximately six hundred thousand Indian Americans, making our Asian Indian population the largest in the Western Hemisphere. A majority of the South Asian residents live in Queens, where nearly one in ten residents is South Asian. The Little India in Jackson Heights is one of the biggest in the city, with a wide variety of different South Asian cuisines and specialty shops.

Seven
FARMER'S
MARKET

Farmers' markets can be found all over New York City, every day of the week. Vendors from Connecticut, New Jersey, Pennsylvania, Long Island, and upstate drive into the City in the predawn hours and are setting up their stands as the sun rises. One of the largest markets is in Union Square, where you can get all kinds of fresh produce, baked goods, freshly cut flowers, and other food items. We love shopping at farmers' markets, picking out what looks freshest that day, and then coming home to create a meal based on the day's purchases. Many of the same vendors go to different markets that pop up in different parts of the City on different days of the week. Though CSAs and farm shares have become popular ways for New Yorkers to get fresh produce, there is still nothing like walking through a New York City farmers' market.

Ethan: *My father's parents were Hungarian immigrants to New York City in the late 1920s, escaping Europe just before the rise of the Nazi Party in Germany and the subsequent Holocaust. Like many Eastern European Jewish immigrants to the Bronx, they were poor skilled laborers. My grandmother, Regina, was known for her exceptional talent in cooking and baking. Her potatoes paprikash are legendary among all who ever had the pleasure of eating at her table.*

POTATOES PAPRIKASH

Serves 4 to 6

1/4 cup canola oil or other neutral oil
1 large yellow onion, cut into 1/4-inch pieces
6 medium red potatoes, peeled and cut into 1/2-inch pieces
1 tablespoon Hungarian paprika
1 teaspoon salt
1/2 cup vegetable broth

1. In a medium nonstick saucepan, heat the oil over medium-high heat. Add the onion and cook, stirring frequently, until browned, about 8 minutes.

2. Lower the heat to medium. Add the potatoes, paprika, and salt, and vigorously mix for 2 minutes. Be sure to scrape the bottom of the pot to keep the mixture from burning. You can add a few tablespoons of water to help prevent sticking. Add the vegetable broth and mix well. Reduce the heat to a simmer, cover, and cook for 20 minutes, stirring frequently, or until the potatoes are fork-tender.

Roasting brings out a sweetness in asparagus that you cannot get from boiling or steaming. This recipe is easily doubled or tripled for those times when you are having company (or just want more asparagus). Try serving this with some Hollandaise Sauce (page 82) to make it fancy.

ROASTED ASPARAGUS

Serves 4

1 pound asparagus, tough ends trimmed
2 teaspoons extra-virgin olive oil
Salt and ground black pepper, to taste
1 tablespoon lemon zest

1. Preheat the oven to 375°F. Line an 18 x 12-inch baking sheet with aluminum foil and set aside.

2. Place the asparagus spears on the prepared baking sheet and toss them with the oil. Spread them out so they are in one layer. Sprinkle the asparagus lightly with the salt and pepper.

3. Roast the asparagus for 20 minutes or until tender and starting to brown. Remove the asparagus from the oven, sprinkle it with the lemon zest, and serve hot.

We don't love the word "wilted," but we do love what wilting does to kale. While "wilted" suggests that something has become lifeless, limp, and devoid of vitality, nothing could be less true of this recipe. Wilting gently softens the kale, making it less bitter while retaining the flavor. The lemon and olive oil add just the right amount of brightness and depth of flavor that rounds out this dish. We love the versatility of this preparation of kale. It pairs beautifully as an accompaniment to a casserole like our Shepherdless Pie (page 90), and it's spectacular with any Italian dish.

WILTED KALE

Serves 4

2 large bunches kale
2 tablespoons extra-virgin olive oil
1 large yellow onion, thinly sliced
2 garlic cloves, minced
1/2 cup vegetable broth
2 tablespoons soy sauce

1. Wash the kale, but do not dry it. Remove the tough stems and coarsely chop the leaves. Set aside. (Save the stems for adding to smoothies or juicing—they are full of kaley goodness.)

2. Heat the oil in a large, heavy pot over medium-high heat. Add the onion and cook for 6 minutes, stirring occasionally, until the onion is soft and just starting to brown.

3. Add the garlic and cook for 30 seconds. Add the kale, vegetable broth, and soy sauce. Cook, stirring often, until the kale has wilted and become tender, 7 to 10 minutes. Transfer the cooked kale to a serving plate and serve hot.

Ethan: *Latkes, the Yiddish word for potato pancakes, are traditionally eaten by Ashkenazic Jews on Hanukkah. You can find latkes at just about any Jewish deli in the city. This recipe is adapted from my Hungarian grandmother, Regina. She insisted that the potatoes and onions must be hand-grated on a box grater and she never used a food processor. I have made these both ways and must admit they come out better when hand-grated. She believed it was the love you put into the food that made it taste better. My father and his brother like to eat these with ketchup, but Michael and I like them with applesauce or vegan sour cream. However you decide to serve your latkes, be sure to serve them fresh out of the skillet as they really should be eaten immediately after frying.*

LATKES

Makes 24 latkes

4 1/2 teaspoons Ener-G Egg Replacer
6 tablespoons warm water
6 large red potatoes, peeled and shredded
1 medium yellow onion, shredded
1 teaspoon salt
Dash ground black pepper
1 cup matzoh meal
Canola oil or other neutral oil, for frying

1. In a small bowl, whisk together the egg replacer and water until fully combined.

2. In a large mixing bowl, add the potatoes, onion, salt, pepper, matzoh meal, and the egg replacer mixture. Mix well by hand to thoroughly combine.

3. Heat 1/4 inch of oil in a large skillet over medium-high heat to 375°F. While the oil is heating, form the potato mixture into compact patties, using about 3 tablespoons per latke. When the oil is heated, fry the latkes in batches, no more than 4 or 5 at time—do not overcrowd the skillet. Fry the latkes for 2 to 3 minutes, or until golden around the edges. Flip them with a spatula and cook the second side until lightly browned.

4. Transfer the cooked latkes to a plate lined with paper towels. Repeat this process until all the latkes are fried, being sure to watch the oil level and adding more as necessary.

Tip: It's really important when making these to be conscious of the size of the latke. If you make them too large, they won't hold together as well and will fall apart when you flip them.

With just a few simple ingredients, cauliflower can become a showstopper at any meal. We love to serve this with our Brisket of Seitan (page 100). Even people who claim not to like cauliflower will love this dish, so be sure to double or even triple the recipe.

ROASTED CAULIFLOWER

Serves 4 to 6

2 tablespoons extra-virgin olive oil
2 teaspoons minced fresh rosemary
1 1/2 teaspoons salt
1/4 teaspoon ground black pepper
20 cloves garlic, peeled and lightly crushed
2 large heads cauliflower, trimmed, cut into bite-size pieces, washed, and left wet

1. Preheat the oven to 450°F. In a large bowl, mix together the oil, rosemary, salt, pepper, and garlic. Add the cauliflower and toss to evenly coat.

2. Spread the cauliflower in a single layer in a 9 x 13-inch baking dish. Roast the cauliflower for 20 minutes, toss, then roast for 10 minutes longer.

There is nothing that says autumn quite like roasted root veggies. This colorful array of vibrant roots and tubers always brightens up a dinner table. When we serve this, people always assume this is difficult to make because of how beautiful it looks and how flavorful it tastes. The truth is, it's a very simple dish to make. The roasting does most of the work by caramelizing the natural sugars in the vegetables.

ROASTED ROOT VEGETABLES

Serves 6 to 8

5 large red beets, peeled and cut into 1-inch pieces
5 large golden beets, peeled and cut into 1-inch pieces
5 large carrots, peeled and cut into 1-inch pieces
10 cloves garlic, peeled
2 large onions, peeled and quartered
2 tablespoons extra-virgin olive oil
1 teaspoon salt, plus more to taste
1/2 teaspoon ground black pepper

1. Preheat the oven to 375°F. Line a 9 x 13-inch roasting pan with aluminum foil and set aside.

2. Put all the red beets, golden beets, carrots, garlic, and onions into a large mixing bowl. Add the oil to the bowl and toss to coat the vegetables. Transfer the vegetables to the prepared roasting pan and sprinkle with the salt and pepper.

3. Roast the vegetables for 20 minutes. After 20 minutes, toss the vegetables and roast another 25 minutes or until the beets are tender. Add a little more salt before serving and serve warm.

Michael: *In the summer, farmers' markets in New York City are overflowing with fresh zucchini, but there's only so much zucchini bread and zoodles a vegan can make! This recipe makes perfect use of those summer-fresh zucchini. My mother, a Brooklyn native, used to make a version of this as an appetizer for guests when entertaining. To me, it was a "fancy" appetizer that always looked very impressive. While my mom used white button mushrooms and a lot of dairy, I prefer this vegan version with cremini mushrooms for their greater depth of flavor and earthiness.*

MUSHROOM-STUFFED ZUCCHINI

Serves 4 to 8

2 cups No-Cook Tomato Sauce (page 83) or store-bought marinara sauce
4 medium zucchini
2 garlic cloves, minced
2 medium tomatoes, seeded and finely chopped
1 cup finely chopped cremini mushrooms
1 teaspoon dried basil
1/2 teaspoon dried oregano
1/4 teaspoon red pepper flakes
2 tablespoons extra-virgin olive oil
3/4 cup Cashew Parmesan (page 16) or store-bought nondairy Parmesan, divided
2 tablespoons finely chopped fresh basil

1. Preheat the oven to 400°F. Spread the tomato sauce on the bottom of a 9 x 13-inch baking dish and set aside

2. Cut the zucchini in half lengthwise. Using a spoon, scoop out the pulp and seeds, leaving a 1/4-inch thick shell. Transfer the zucchini shells to the baking dish, cut-side up. Chop up the pulp from the zucchini and place it into a large mixing bowl.

3. Add the garlic, tomatoes, mushrooms, basil, oregano, red pepper flakes, oil, and 1/2 cup of the cashew Parmesan to the bowl with the zucchini pulp. Mix well. Spoon the mixture into the zucchini shells.

4. Cover the baking dish with aluminum foil. Bake for 25 minutes, or until the zucchini are tender. After 25 minutes, uncover the baking dish and bake for 5 minutes longer. Remove the zucchini from the oven. Top them with the fresh basil and remaining 1/4 cup cashew Parmesan and serve warm.

Michael: *As a child, I didn't care for spinach, but as an adult, I have come to really enjoy it—especially when it's creamed. My mother used to serve this with roasted meats, but we find that it pairs quite nicely with our Brisket of Seitan (page 100) and our Southern-Fried Seitan (page 107).*

CREAMED SPINACH

Serves 4

1 tablespoon canola oil or other neutral oil
2 medium shallots, finely chopped
2 cloves garlic, minced
2 tablespoons unbleached all-purpose flour
2 tablespoons nutritional yeast
1 cup plain unsweetened almond milk
1/4 teaspoon ground nutmeg
1/2 teaspoon salt
1/4 teaspoon ground black pepper
1 1/2 pounds fresh spinach, rinsed and roughly chopped

1. In a large skillet, heat the oil over medium heat. Add the shallots and cook until they are translucent, about 6 minutes. Add the garlic and cook 1 minute or until fragrant. Add the flour and nutritional yeast. Cook, stirring constantly, for 1 minute.

2. Whisk in the almond milk. Add the nutmeg, salt, and pepper, and continue to whisk. Raise the heat to high and cook, whisking constantly, until the mixture is thickened, about 2 minutes. Add the spinach, stir, and cook until it is tender, 4 to 5 minutes. Serve immediately.

Acorn squash are naturally filled with complex sugars that caramelize in the roasting process. This recipe makes use of that sweetness, but we add some nondairy butter, maple syrup, and brown sugar to really make it pop. This is a great side dish for a Thanksgiving meal and the presentation of the halved squash with a browned-butter filled cavity is always striking.

ROASTED ACORN SQUASH

Serves 4

2 medium acorn squash
2 tablespoons nondairy butter
2 tablespoons brown sugar
2 tablespoons maple syrup
Pinch salt

1. Preheat the oven to 375°F. Line a 9 x 13-inch roasting pan with aluminum foil and set aside.

2. Slice each squash in half horizontally and scoop out the seeds. Slice the pointy tip off the bottom half, being careful not to cut into the cavity in the squash. You want to cut off just enough to enable the squash to stand up. Place the 4 squash halves in the roasting pan cut-side up.

3. In a small bowl, combine the butter, brown sugar, maple syrup, and salt. Spread the mixture all over the cut sides of the squash. Once they are all coated, add the remaining sugar mixture equally into the cavity of each squash half. Bake the squash for 40 minutes or until the flesh is easily pierced with a paring knife. Remove the squash from the oven and allow them to cool for a few minutes before serving.

Saint Patrick's Day in New York City is a bigger, more celebrated holiday than it is in Ireland. It's an Irish Pride Day of sorts, and in New York City, everybody is a little bit Irish that day. After watching the parade and hanging with friends at your favorite Irish pub, go home and fill up on this traditional Irish dish.

COLCANNON

Serves 6 to 8

6 Yukon gold potatoes, peeled and cut into 1-inch pieces
1 tablespoon extra-virgin olive oil
1 shallot, finely chopped
2 cloves garlic, minced
1 leek, thoroughly washed and cut into 1/4-inch thick slices (white and light green parts)
1 large bunch kale, tough stems removed, washed, and finely chopped
2 teaspoons soy sauce
1/2 teaspoon liquid smoke
2 tablespoons nondairy butter
1/3 cup plain unsweetened almond milk, warmed
1 tablespoon nutritional yeast
Salt and ground black pepper, to taste

1. Place the potatoes in a large pot and cover them with 1 inch of cold water. Turn the heat to high and bring the potatoes to a boil. Once the potatoes come to a boil, turn the heat to medium-low, and boil the potatoes until fork-tender, 15 to 20 minutes. Drain the potatoes in a colander.

2. Return the potatoes to the pot and put it back on the stove at medium heat for a minute or two to dry them out. Reduce the heat to low to keep the potatoes warm until you need them.

3. While the potatoes are boiling, heat the oil in a large skillet or shallow pot over medium-high heat. Add the shallot and sauté for 2 minutes to soften. Add the garlic and sauté 30 seconds or until just golden. Add the leek and sauté 5 minutes or until soft. Add the kale and soy sauce. Cook the kale until it is soft and reduced, about 1 minute. Add the liquid smoke. Stir well.

4. Add the potatoes to the kale mixture and mash roughly with a potato masher. Add the butter, milk, and nutritional yeast. Mix well. Add the salt and pepper to taste.

Ethan: *Neither of us grew up with any exposure to Southern or Caribbean food. That all changed for me when I was in medical school. There is a fabulous Caribbean soul food restaurant next door to the clinic where I worked in East Harlem, and they serve up all sorts of foods I'd never seen before. I always ordered the vegetarian platter: roti, curry potatoes, collard greens, callaloo, and okra.*

CARIBBEAN-STYLE CALLALOO WITH OKRA

Serves 4

2 tablespoons canola oil or other neutral oil
1 medium onion, cut into 1/2-inch pieces
1 medium tomato, coarsely chopped
2 green onions, finely chopped
1/2 red bell pepper, cut into 1/2-inch pieces
1/4 teaspoon dried thyme
3 cloves garlic, minced
2 pounds water spinach, collard greens, Swiss chard, or mustard greens, tough stems removed
5 okra pods, cut diagonally into 1/4-inch thick slices
1/4 cup water
Salt and ground black pepper, to taste

1. Heat the oil in a large skillet over medium heat. Add the onion, tomato, green onions, bell pepper, and thyme and sauté for 4 minutes. Add the garlic and sauté for 1 more minute.

2. Add the greens, okra, water, and salt and pepper. Cover the skillet and simmer on low heat for 15 minutes or until the vegetables are tender.

Caribbean Culture

Brooklyn is the home to West Indians of every nationality. In the 1960s, Jamaicans began arriving in the Flatbush section of Brooklyn, attracted by jobs as healthcare workers at Kings County Hospital. Soon, Haitian immigrants followed suit. Around the same time, the nearby neighborhoods of Crown Heights and Bedford Stuyvesant saw an influx of people from Trinidad, Barbados, and Guyana. While the influence of Caribbean culture can be found in restaurants all around the City—many pizza places now sell Jamaican jerk patties—for truly authentic West Indian food in New York, a trip to Brooklyn is a must.

In the middle of the summer, when farmers' markets are overflowing with cucumbers and tomatoes, we love to stock up and make a big bowl of Israeli Salad to enjoy throughout the week. You can enjoy it on its own or pair it with some Falafel (page 63), Hummus (page 75), and Spiced Carrots (page 130) for a Middle Eastern feast.

ISRAELI SALAD

Serves 6

6 medium Roma tomatoes, seeded and cut into 1/4-inch pieces
1 English cucumber or 4 Persian cucumbers, cut into 1/4-inch pieces
1/4 medium red onion, cut into 1/4-inch pieces
2 tablespoons finely chopped fresh parsley
2 tablespoons extra-virgin olive oil
Salt and ground black pepper, to taste
Juice of 1 lemon

1. Combine the tomatoes, cucumber, onion, and parsley in a large bowl. Toss well.

2. Add the oil and salt and pepper. Toss well. Add the lemon juice, 1 teaspoon at a time, tossing after each addition, tasting after each addition until the desired level of tartness is achieved. Serve immediately.

"And New York is the most beautiful city in the world? It is not far from it. No urban night is like the night there. . . . Squares after squares of flame, set up and cut into the aether. Here is our poetry, for we have pulled down the stars to our will."

— Ezra Pound

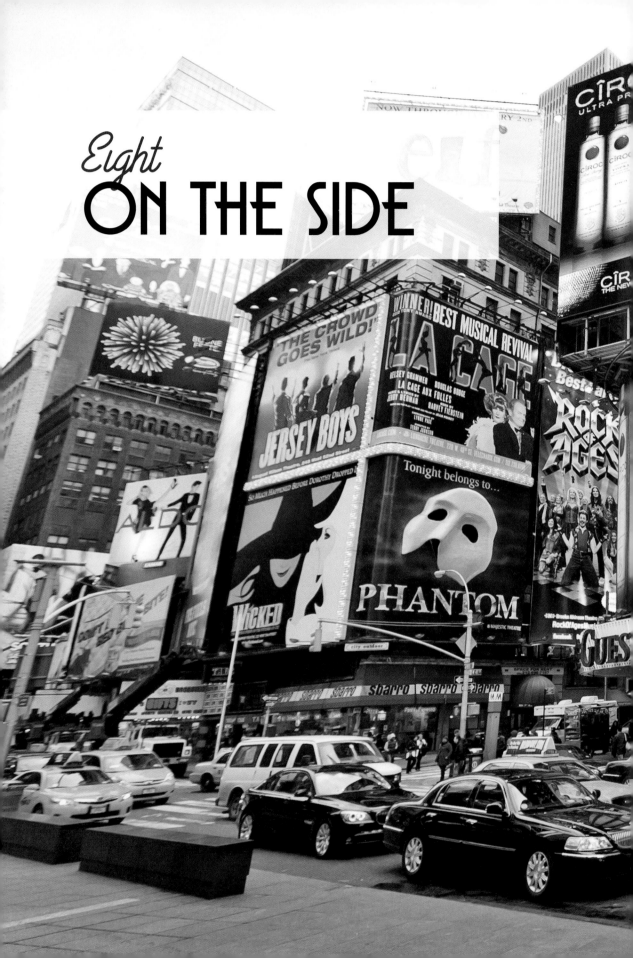

Eight
ON THE SIDE

Much of life in New York City is about what side you're on. Mia was on the East Side while Woody was on the West. But being from the City is more than simply claiming areas on a map. For many New Yorkers, it is a more defining question: Mets or Yankees? We're a mixed marriage: Michael's family are Mets fans, but Ethan's family are Yankees fans, as his dad was born in the Bronx. Michael's mother is still waiting for the Dodgers to return to her native Brooklyn. For vegans, the question can be far more significant: Candle Café, East or West? Seriously, though, we're calling these recipes "sides," but in truth, they can combine together in the spirit of a meze platter and become a meal unto themselves.

In 2013, Dominicans became the largest Latino population in New York City, surpassing Puerto Ricans. Versions of this dish, which literally translates to "rice with corn," can be found in Cuban and Puerto Rican cuisine, but we prefer it Dominican-style using Goya brand sazón seasoning. Leftovers can be shaped into patties and pan-fried in a little oil for a delicious lunch.

ARROZ CON MAIZ

Serves 4 to 6

2 tablespoons extra-virgin olive oil
1 large yellow onion, cut into 1/4-inch pieces
1 medium red bell pepper, cut into 1/4-inch pieces
3 cloves garlic, minced
1 cup No-Cook Tomato Sauce (page 83) or store-bought marinara sauce
2 dried bay leaves
2 cups long-grain white rice
1 envelope Goya brand sazón seasoning blend
1/4 cup white wine
1 teaspoon fresh lemon juice
3 1/2 cups vegetable broth
1 cup canned corn, drained, or 1 1/2 cups frozen sweet corn
Salt and ground black pepper, to taste

1. Heat the oil in a large saucepan over medium heat. Add the onion, bell pepper, and garlic and cook for 5 to 7 minutes, stirring occasionally, until the onion is translucent. Be careful not to brown the onion. Add the tomato sauce and bay leaves. Cook for 5 minutes.

2. Add the rice and stir well. Add the sazón, white wine, lemon juice, and vegetable broth. Stir well to combine. Stir in the corn and bring the mixture to a boil. Reduce the heat to low, cover the pan, and cook for about 20 minutes, or until the rice is tender and all the liquid is absorbed. Taste the rice and season to taste with the salt and pepper.

Dominican Communities

Though Dominicans have been immigrating to New York since the late nineteenth century, the large wave of immigration began in earnest in the 1960s, after the death of dictator Rafael Trujillo. Followed by the invasion of Santo Domingo and the regime of Joaquín Balaguer, Dominicans rapidly became the largest group of immigrants to New York City from the 1970s through the 1990s. There are vibrant Dominican communities throughout the city, particularly in northern Manhattan and the south Bronx. Today, one in four Latinos in New York City is Dominican.

Ethan: *Our little Chihuahua, Phoebe (who inspired the Fruit Smoothie on page 38), was the driving force behind this salad. I rescued her from the Manhattan Animal Care Center, New York's high-kill shelter in East Harlem. She was found abandoned and chained to a radiator when her original family moved out and left her behind. Thankfully, I was at the shelter looking for a companion for my other dog, Blackie, when she was brought in, barely alive. Being a tough New York City dog, she fought back and made a full recovery. Once when she was having stomach issues, we had to find a "novel" protein for her and gave her this mix of lentils, quinoa, and carrots, and she loved it. We then realized that even though this was originally intended to be "dog food," it was really a delicious dish.*

PHOEBE'S SALAD

Serves 6 to 8

1 cup green lentils
6 cups vegetable broth, divided
1 tablespoon extra-virgin olive oil
1 cup quinoa
2 large carrots, peeled and cut into 1/4-inch pieces
1 clove garlic, smashed
Salt and ground black pepper, to taste

1. Combine the lentils and 4 cups of the vegetable broth in a large saucepan. If the lentils aren't covered with the broth, add water until they are covered by 1 inch. Bring the lentils to a boil and then reduce the heat to simmer. Cook, uncovered, 20 to 30 minutes, until the lentils are soft. Drain the lentils and transfer them to a large mixing bowl.

2. While the lentils are cooking, prepare the quinoa. If your quinoa isn't pre-washed, place it in a strainer and rinse it well, until the water runs clear. (If you don't rinse unwashed quinoa, it can be bitter.) Transfer the rinsed quinoa to a medium saucepan. Add the remaining 2 cups vegetable broth, cover, and bring the quinoa to a boil. Once boiling, reduce the heat to a simmer and cook for 15 minutes, or until all the broth is absorbed.

3. Heat the oil in a medium skillet over medium-high heat. Add the carrots and garlic and sauté until the carrots are soft but not mushy, about 6 minutes. Add the cooked quinoa and carrots to the lentils. Season with the salt and pepper. Mix well and serve hot.

The Dogs of New York

We couldn't mention our beloved rescue Chihuahua, Phoebe, and not talk about the dogs of New York City. The City is home to over six hundred thousand dogs. Considering the large number of apartments that do not allow pets, this is huge. You can find pretty much every variety of dog living in New York City, from purebreds to mutts. If you want to get a companion animal in New York City, we hope you'll visit the Animal Care Centers of NYC and save a life. Each year in the five boroughs of New York, the city euthanizes over six thousand animals. Please remember: adopt, don't shop. The group's web address is https://www.nycacc.org/.

Go to any kosher deli or diner in New York City, order a sandwich, and it will arrive with a small dish of coleslaw topped with a pickle spear on the side, whether you want it or not. Ethan's mother taught us this recipe, having gotten it from her mother in law. Serve this coleslaw on the side of our Tempeh Reuben (page 59), and you will feel like you are eating at Carnegie Deli. Oh, and don't forget the pickle (recipe opposite).

COLESLAW

Serves 6 to 8

1 medium head cabbage, washed and quartered
3 medium carrots, peeled
1 small green bell pepper, quartered
1 1/2 cups nondairy mayonnaise
1/4 cup apple cider vinegar
2 tablespoons fresh lemon juice
1/4 cup sugar

1. Using the slicing surface of a box grater, shred the cabbage into a large mixing bowl. (Be careful not to shred any of the hard white core, as it is very bitter.)

2. Using the shredding surface of the box grater, shred the carrots into the bowl with the cabbage.

3. Using the shredding surface of the box grater, shred only the flesh of the bell pepper into the bowl with the cabbage and carrots. Be careful to not shred any of the skin. Set the bowl aside.

4. In a small mixing bowl, whisk together the mayonnaise, apple cider vinegar, lemon juice, and sugar. If the dressing is too thick, you can thin it out with a few tablespoons of water.

5. Pour the dressing over the shredded vegetables and mix well. You can serve this immediately, but it tastes even better after being allowed to chill, covered, in the refrigerator for a few hours to overnight. Store any leftovers covered in the refrigerator for up to 4 days.

"On the side is very big with you."

—Harry Burns to Sally Albright, *When Harry Met Sally*

Izzy Guss, a Polish Jewish immigrant to New York City, settled in the Lower East Side in 1910. When he opened the now famous Guss' Pickles, there were eighty other pickle stores in the neighborhood. Nearly a century later, Guss' is the only one left standing. Their motto is "Imitated but never duplicated," and that is true because their unique old-world recipe makes their pickles truly one of a kind. This recipe is our homage to them because, let's face it, imitation is the sincerest form of flattery.

HALF-SOUR PICKLES

Makes 2 quarts

2 pounds Kirby cucumbers (also known as pickling cucumbers)
4 cups water
1/4 cup kosher salt
1/2 teaspoon coriander seeds
1/2 teaspoon mustard seeds
1/2 teaspoon allspice berries
1/2 teaspoon black peppercorns
3 dried bay leaves
6 cloves garlic, crushed
2 sprigs fresh dill

1. Wash the cucumbers well and set aside. Thoroughly wash 2 widemouthed 1-quart mason jars or 1 half-gallon mason jar with hot soapy water and rinse well.

2. Combine the water and salt in a large bowl and stir until the salt is completely dissolved. Set aside.

3. In a sealable plastic bag, combine the coriander seeds, mustard seeds, allspice berries, peppercorns, and bay leaves. Use a rolling pin to crush the spices. You don't want them finely ground, just crushed.

4. Place 3 cloves garlic, 1 sprig of dill, and half of the spice mixture into each Mason jar.

5. Put the cucumbers into the jars and pack them as tightly as you can. If the cucumbers are thick, you may have to slice them in half lengthwise or even quarter them.

6. Pour enough salt water into each jar to cover the cucumbers.

7. Cover the jars and refrigerate for at least 5 days before eating. These will keep in the refrigerator for a few weeks.

In New York, there is an abundance of falafel restaurants. Whether Maoz, The Hummus & Pita Co., or your local hole in the wall, vegans have a delicious go-to meal anywhere in the city. At Maoz, we order our falafel with our favorite topping, spiced carrots. Anytime we make our Falafel (page 63) at home, we are sure to make these.

SPICED CARROTS

Serves 4 to 6

1 pound carrots, peeled and cut into 1/4-inch thick rounds
2 cups water
2 cloves garlic, minced
2 tablespoons extra-virgin olive oil
1/2 teaspoon paprika
1 pinch cayenne pepper, or to taste
Salt and ground black pepper, to taste
1 tablespoon red wine vinegar
1/2 teaspoon ground cumin

1. Combine the carrots, water, garlic, oil, paprika, cayenne pepper, salt and black pepper in a medium skillet. Bring the carrots to a boil over medium-high heat and cook until the carrots are tender and the water evaporates, about 20 minutes.

2. Add the vinegar and cumin to the carrot mixture and toss to evenly coat the carrots. Remove the skillet from the heat and set aside to allow the carrots to cool to room temperature before serving.

"Everybody ought to have a Lower East Side in their life."

— Irving Berlin

Summer in New York City means weekend street fairs. When we were first dating, one of our favorite summer weekend activities was hitting street fairs. Unlike most fairs, these fairs do not have rides or games. Instead, avenues are closed to traffic for several blocks, and vendors selling everything from tube socks to works of art line the street. In addition to the things for sale, there are always dozens of food vendors. One of the most popular food stands is the one selling Mexican Street Corn—freshly grilled sweet corn coated in a mixture of cheese and spiced mayonnaise. We created a vegan version of this dish that tastes even better than the original.

STREET FAIR CORN

Serves 4

1/4 cup nondairy mayonnaise
1/4 cup nondairy sour cream
1/4 cup Cashew Parmesan (page 16) or store bought nondairy parmesan, plus more for serving
1/2 teaspoon chili powder, plus more for serving
1 medium clove garlic, finely minced
1 tablespoon finely chopped fresh cilantro or Italian parsley
4 ears sweet corn, shucked
1 lime, cut into wedges

1. Heat a grill for direct-heat grilling, or heat a grill pan over high heat on the stove. While the grill is heating, in a medium mixing bowl, combine the mayonnaise, sour cream, cashew parmesan, chili powder, garlic, and cilantro. Stir until completely combined.

2. Place the corn directly on the hot grill and cook, rotating occasionally, until cooked through and charred in spots on all sides, about 8 minutes total.

3. Remove the corn from the grill and transfer to a serving plate. Use a pastry or basting brush to generously coat each ear of corn with the mayonnaise mixture. Sprinkle with extra cheese and chili powder and serve immediately with lime wedges.

Anytime you go out for Chinese food in New York, you'll find a few pieces of steamed broccoli placed as a garnish alongside your entrée. As vegans, we always want more than the little amount served. In this recipe, we kick simple steamed broccoli up a few notches by adding garlic, ginger, and sesame. Even people who claim not to like broccoli love this dish.

SESAME BROCCOLI

Serves 4

1 tablespoon sesame seeds
1/2 cup vegetable broth
1 tablespoon soy sauce (use wheat-free soy sauce for a gluten-free option)
1 1/2 teaspoons dark sesame oil
1 tablespoon plus 1 teaspoon canola oil or other neutral oil, divided
1 pound fresh broccoli florets, rinsed, patted dry, and cut into bite-size pieces
2 cloves garlic, minced
1 tablespoon minced fresh ginger

1. Heat a small nonstick skillet over medium heat. Add the sesame seeds and gently shake the pan so they spread out in a single layer. Let the seeds cook until lightly browned, stirring occasionally, 3 to 5 minutes. Do not walk away from them while cooking, as once they start to brown they can easily burn. Once the seeds are lightly toasted, remove them from the heat, transfer them to a small bowl, and set aside.

2. Combine the vegetable broth, soy sauce, and dark sesame oil in a small bowl. Mix well and set aside.

3. Heat 1 tablespoon of the canola oil in a large skillet over medium-high heat. Add the broccoli florets and toss to coat the florets with the oil. Sauté the broccoli for about 1 minute. Move the broccoli to the sides of the skillet and add the remaining 1 teaspoon of canola oil, garlic, and ginger to the center of the pan. Sauté the garlic and ginger for 30 seconds, and then stir in the broccoli to combine.

4. Add the vegetable broth mixture to the skillet. Bring the mixture to a simmer, then reduce the heat to medium-low and cover the skillet. Cook for 2 to 3 minutes, until the broccoli is still firm but can be pierced with a fork. Remove the skillet from the heat. Transfer the broccoli to a medium bowl with a slotted spoon. Return the skillet to the stove, increase the heat to high, and boil down the liquid until 2 tablespoons remain. Turn off the heat, return the broccoli to the pan, add the toasted sesame seeds, and toss the broccoli and seeds with the liquid. Transfer the sesame broccoli to a serving bowl and serve hot.

Michael: *Hands down, the best fries we have had in New York are at the all-vegan Champs Diner in Brooklyn. They arrive in a large basket, piping hot and perfectly crispy. After much trial and error, we learned the tricks to making perfectly crispy fries at home: a cold water bath and frying the potatoes twice.*

FRENCH FRIES

Serves 4

4 large russet potatoes
4 cups canola oil or other neutral oil, for frying
Salt, to taste

1. Fill a large bowl with ice water. Peel the potatoes (or, if leaving the skin on, scrub them thoroughly). Cut the potatoes into strips as thin or thick as you like; we like them about 1/4-inch thick. Put the potatoes into the ice water and refrigerate at least 30 minutes.

2. Drain the potatoes and thoroughly pat them dry. Heat the oil in a large pot over medium-high heat to 350°F. Make sure you have at least 2 inches of space between the top of the oil and the rim of the pot.

3. Add a handful of fries to the oil and fry, stirring occasionally, for about 10 minutes, until they are soft and limp. (Don't worry, you will be getting them crispy later.) Remove the potatoes from the oil with a slotted spoon and transfer them to a paper towel–lined plate to drain. Repeat this process with the remaining fries, one handful at a time, until they are all fried. Let the potatoes rest for at least 10 minutes. Turn off the heat.

4. When you are ready to serve the fries, reheat the oil to 350°F. Place all the fries in the oil and fry again, stirring frequently. Cook until they are golden brown, or even longer if you prefer them darker, about 7 minutes. Remove the fries from the oil with a slotted spoon or sieve and transfer them to paper towels to drain. Sprinkle with salt and serve with your favorite condiments, such as ketchup, nondairy mayonnaise, or malt vinegar.

"New York City is where specks of dust aspire randomly with all their cunning to become grains of sand."

— David B. Lentz, *The Fine Art of Grace: A Novel*

With the tomatoes, pasta, and peas, this dish looks like an Italian flag on your plate. We love to serve this alongside our Seitan Piccata (page 95). You can also toss it with a little Italian dressing for a wonderful pasta salad.

ORZO WITH PEAS AND TOASTED PINE NUTS

Serves 8 to 10

4 cups vegetable broth
2 cups water
16 ounces orzo
1/3 cup pine nuts
1 tablespoon extra-virgin olive oil
1 clove garlic, minced
2 large Roma tomatoes, coarsely chopped
1 cup frozen peas
Salt and ground black pepper, to taste
1/2 cup Cashew Parmesan (page 16) or store-bought nondairy Parmesan

1. In a large saucepan, bring the vegetable broth and water to a boil over high heat. Add the orzo and cook until tender but still firm to the bite, stirring occasionally, 8 to 10 minutes.

2. While the pasta is cooking, heat a large skillet over medium-high heat and add the pine nuts. After a minute or two, the nuts should begin to turn golden. Shake the pan continually to toss the nuts to prevent them from burning. When the nuts are golden, transfer them from the skillet to a small bowl.

3. Return the skillet to the stove and heat the oil over medium-high heat. Add the garlic and cook for 1 minute. Add the tomatoes and cook until heated through, about 2 minutes.

4. Put the frozen peas in a colander and drain the orzo over the peas, reserving 1/2 cup of the cooking liquid. Transfer the orzo and peas to a large serving bowl. Add the cooked tomatoes and pine nuts, and season with salt and pepper. Toss well to combine, adding the reserved cooking liquid to loosen the pasta if needed. Top with the cashew Parmesan and serve hot.

Michael: *The first time I had onion straws was when I was about eight years old and my family went to a barbecue restaurant in New York City for dinner. One of the restaurant's side dishes was an onion loaf—a loaf of fried onions. The only time I ever had onions prepared like this was at this one restaurant. For many reasons, that is not a restaurant I will be returning to. However, I can have a version of their onion loaf anytime I want it.*

ONION LOAF

Serves 6 to 8

1 cup plain unsweetened nondairy milk
1 teaspoon apple cider vinegar
1 cup rice flour
1 cup unbleached all-purpose flour
2 teaspoons salt
2 large onions, thinly sliced and separated into rings
4 cups canola oil or other neutral oil, for frying
Kosher salt, to taste

1. Mix the milk and vinegar together in a small cup and set aside for 10 minutes.

2. Combine the rice flour, all-purpose flour, and salt in a large bowl. Whisk to thoroughly combine.

3. Place the onions in a large bowl. Pour the milk mixture over the onions and toss to coat. Let them soak for 30 minutes. After 30 minutes, remove the onions and shake off any excess liquid.

4. Heat the oil in a large pot or electric frying pan to 375°F. Dredge the onions in the flour mixture and toss to coat evenly. Add the onions to the hot oil in small batches and fry until they are crispy, about 2 minutes per batch. Remove the onions from the oil with a slotted spoon and transfer them to a paper towel–lined plate to drain. Season the onions with the kosher salt. Transfer the onions to a 9 x 5-inch loaf pan. Repeat until all the onions are fried and added to the loaf pan. Press the onions down to really pack them in tightly.

5. Invert the loaf pan onto a serving platter and carefully lift the pan up. You should be left with a loaf of perfectly fried onions. If it falls apart, don't worry, it will still be delicious. Serve with your favorite condiments, such as ketchup, barbecue sauce, or ranch dressing.

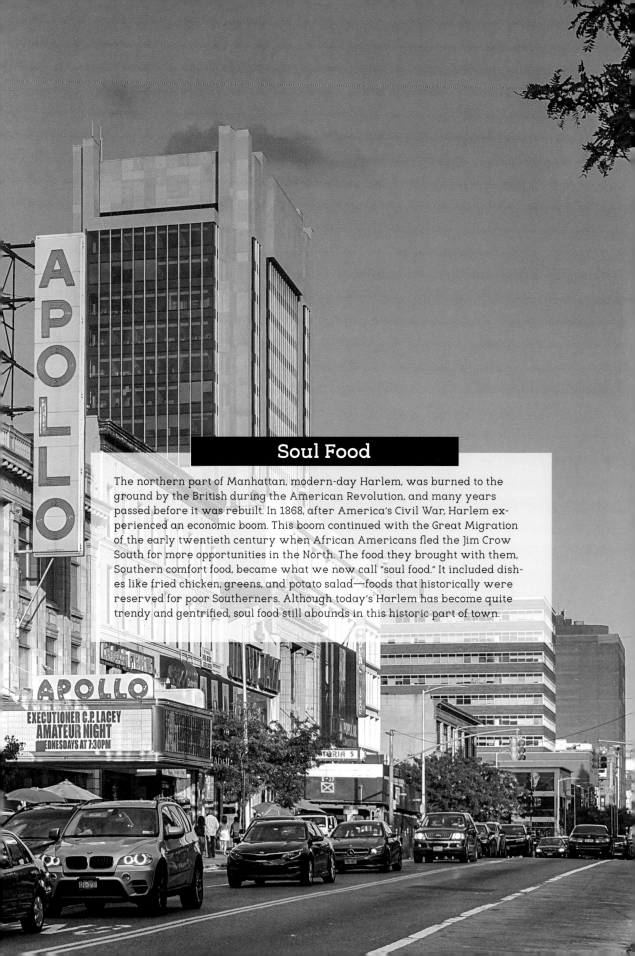

Soul Food

The northern part of Manhattan, modern-day Harlem, was burned to the ground by the British during the American Revolution, and many years passed before it was rebuilt. In 1868, after America's Civil War, Harlem experienced an economic boom. This boom continued with the Great Migration of the early twentieth century when African Americans fled the Jim Crow South for more opportunities in the North. The food they brought with them, Southern comfort food, became what we now call "soul food." It included dishes like fried chicken, greens, and potato salad—foods that historically were reserved for poor Southerners. Although today's Harlem has become quite trendy and gentrified, soul food still abounds in this historic part of town.

Ethan: *When I was in college in Manhattan, I ate a lot of weird stuff. I would combine leftovers of all sorts, trying different mixtures and concoctions. One day, I came back from class starving for lunch, only to realize that the only things I had in the fridge were leftover egg salad, leftover potato salad, and a jar of pimento-stuffed olives. I mixed the salads, added a few olives and a squeeze of mustard, and a new family recipe was born. Soon enough, everyone in my family wanted the recipe for Ethan's Potato Salad. Years later, after I had gone vegan, I was talking to my grandmother one night and she said, "I made your famous potato salad. You probably don't make that anymore, do you?" I said, "You know, Bubby, I haven't made it in a long time, but I'm going to." When she asked me what I would do about the eggs, I said, "Just you wait and see."*

POTATO SALAD

Serves 6 to 8

2 pounds red potatoes
5 ounces extra-firm tofu or super-firm sprouted tofu
1 tablespoon ground turmeric
1 teaspoon black salt
10 pimento-stuffed green olives, halved crosswise
1/2 cup nondairy mayonnaise
2 tablespoons yellow mustard
1 teaspoon paprika
1 teaspoon garlic powder
1 teaspoon onion powder
1/2 teaspoon Himalayan pink salt
1/2 teaspoon ground black pepper

1. Bring a large pot of water to a boil, pierce the potatoes with a fork, and add them to the water. Cover the pot and boil the potatoes for 35 minutes, or until fork-tender. Drain the potatoes and set aside to cool.

2. While the potatoes are boiling, add the tofu to a large mixing bowl and mash it with a fork. Add the turmeric and black salt and mix very well. Set aside.

3. Peel the potatoes and coarsely chop them into 1-inch cubes. Transfer the cubed potatoes to the bowl with the tofu. Add the olives to the bowl and mix well.

4. In a small bowl, combine the mayonnaise, mustard, paprika, garlic powder, onion powder, pink salt, and pepper. Mix to thoroughly combine. Use a large mixing spoon or spatula to fold this dressing into the potato mixture. Take your time and make sure everything gets evenly coated. It is okay if some potatoes fall apart during the mixing. Adjust the seasonings to your taste and serve.

Note: Whether you serve this immediately at room temperature or you let it chill covered in the refrigerator for a few hours, it will taste fantastic. It is really an issue of personal tastes. Store leftovers, covered, in the refrigerator for up to 3 days.

Nine
HOW SWEET IT IS

New Yorkers love their sweets! Whether you prefer a classic French-style patisserie, an old-world Italian bakery, or sweet treats from street carts, there is always an abundance of delicious desserts waiting for you on every block. In New York City, you can tell the ethnicity of a neighborhood by its bakeries. While gentrification has taken its toll on many neighborhood bakeries, you can still find ethnic bakeries throughout the City. For example, if you travel east on Coney Island Avenue in Brooklyn, from Prospect Park out to Brighton Beach by the Atlantic Ocean, you will find a Mexican tortilla bakery, Pakistani sweet shops, a kosher bagel bakery, a Turkish bread bakery, a non-kosher bagel bakery, a Middle Eastern pastry shop, and several Russian-Ukrainian bakeries. With each different bakery, you will find yourself in an ethnically different neighborhood than you were in just a block or two before.

For over four years, a woman named Ana Alvarado has been selling churros in subway stations daily during the evening rush from 3:30 p.m. to 7:00 p.m. Sadly, she has been arrested many times for doing this, but still she refuses to stop as the money she makes enables her to support her family. Ana is not the only renegade subway churro vendor in the City; several other women do it as well. We have never been able to ascertain whether their churros are vegan, so we came with our own recipe.

PLATFORM CHURROS

Serves 6 to 8

2 cups water
1/2 cup plus 2 tablespoons sugar, divided
1 teaspoon salt
2 tablespoons canola oil or other neutral oil, plus more for frying
2 cups unbleached all-purpose flour
2 teaspoons ground cinnamon

1. Bring the water to a boil in a medium saucepan over high heat. When the water boils, add 2 tablespoons of the sugar and the salt. Stir until the sugar and salt dissolve. Stir in the oil and remove the pan from the stove. Add the flour to the water mixture and stir until combined and the mixture forms a ball. Carefully transfer the hot mixture into a cookie press with a large star tip.

2. Pour 3 inches of oil into a large pot and heat it over medium-high heat to 375°F. Squeeze 3-inch lengths of the churro batter into the hot oil and fry until they are golden brown. Do not overcrowd the pot—work in small batches to avoid cooling down the oil. Use a slotted spoon to transfer the churros from the oil to a paper towel-lined plate. Repeat this process until all the dough is used.

3. Put the remaining 1/2 cup sugar and cinnamon in a paper bag and shake well to mix. While one batch of churros is cooking, put the cooked churros in the bag with the cinnamon sugar and shake to coat. Repeat this process as you cook more churros. Churros are meant to be eaten almost as soon as they are made. Don't worry about how to store leftovers—you won't have any.

Note: The dough is very stiff, so you will need a cookie press, or churro press if you have one, to pipe the dough into the oil for frying.

Thanks to a famous episode of Seinfeld, the black and white cookie, once only known to New Yorkers, garnered national attention. In that episode, Jerry used the black and white as a metaphor for racial harmony. Although called a cookie, these treats are actually made from a stiff cake batter and baked free-form on a cookie sheet. Once found only in bakeries, today the black and white can be found in almost every grocery store and bodega in New York.

BLACK AND WHITE COOKIES

Makes 18 cookies

Cookies:
2 1/2 cups unbleached all-purpose flour
1 1/4 teaspoons baking powder
1/2 teaspoon baking soda
1/2 teaspoon salt
1 cup sugar
1 cup nondairy butter
1/4 cup Chock Full o' Nuts Milk (page 7) or store-bought nondairy milk, at room temperature
2 teaspoons vanilla extract

Icing:
3 1/2 cups confectioners' sugar
1/4 cup boiling water, plus more if needed
1/4 teaspoon vanilla extract
2/3 cup nondairy semisweet chocolate chips

1. Preheat the oven to 350°F. Line 2 (18 x 12-inch) baking sheets with parchment paper. In a large bowl, whisk together the flour, baking powder, baking soda, and salt. Set aside.

2. In another large bowl, combine the sugar and butter and beat until creamy, about 5 minutes. Add the milk and vanilla and beat until incorporated. Add the flour mixture to the butter mixture in batches, beating after each addition, until combined.

3. Scoop the dough, 1/4 cup at a time, onto the prepared baking sheets, spacing the scoops 3 inches apart. Flatten them slightly with your hands (keep your hands wet to prevent the dough from sticking). Allow room between the scoops as the cookies will spread as they bake.

4. Bake the cookies for 15 minutes or until a toothpick inserted in the center comes out clean. Allow the cookies to cool 2 minutes on the baking sheets and then carefully flip the cookies over and transfer them, upside down, to a wire rack to cool completely.

5. While the cookies are cooling, make the icing. In a large mixing bowl, combine the confectioners' sugar, boiling water, and vanilla. Mix well to get a spreadable icing. Add a little more water, if needed. Using an offset spatula, spread a thin layer of icing onto the flat side, the former bottom, of each cookie. Return the cookies to the wire rack to dry. You should have about 1/2 cup of icing left.

6. While the white icing is drying, melt the chocolate chips in a microwave or double boiler. When the chips are all melted and smooth, whisk the melted chocolate into the remaining

icing. The chocolate icing should be thicker than the white, but still be spreadable. If it is too thick, add a little hot water to thin it out. Use the offset spatula to frost one half of each cookie over the white icing. Return the cookies to the wire racks to dry. Store leftovers in a covered container for up for 5 days.

Ethan: *No New York City-themed cookbook would be complete without a nod to the Big Apple. And no food is more American than apple pie. There isn't a diner in New York City that doesn't have an apple pie waiting to be served. At ninety years young, my grandmother still makes a killer apple pie. Her secret? New York State apples. Growing up, I would climb the apple tree in her backyard and pick the apples, and she'd bake them up into a seemingly effortless pie. To this day, her pie recipe is totally vegan. I've modified her crust recipe by adding the apple cider vinegar to give it a flakier texture.*

BIG APPLE PIE

Serves 8 to 10

Crust:

3 cups unbleached all-purpose flour, plus more for rolling out dough

1/4 cup sugar

1 teaspoon salt

1 cup plus 2 tablespoons vegan shortening

1/2 cup ice water, plus more as needed

4 teaspoons apple cider vinegar

Filling:

5 large Honeycrisp apples (or any red apple you prefer), peeled, cored, and cut into 1/2-inch pieces

1 medium Granny Smith apple, peeled, cored, and cut into 1/2-inch pieces

1 cup sugar

1 tablespoon fresh lemon juice

3/4 cup unbleached all-purpose flour

1 tablespoon ground cinnamon

1/4 teaspoon ground nutmeg

1/8 teaspoon ground allspice, optional

1. In a medium mixing bowl, sift together the flour, sugar, and salt. Cut in the shortening using a fork (or use your fingers like I do) until it is evenly crumbled.

2. Combine the ice water and apple cider vinegar in a glass. Drizzle a small amount over the flour mixture and mix well to moisten. Repeat this process in small increments, pouring more liquid and mixing, until the dough can be pressed into a soft ball. Divide the dough in half and form each half into ball. Flatten each ball into a disk and wrap the disks separately in plastic and refrigerate for at least 1 hour.

3. While the dough is chilling, place the apples in a large mixing bowl, add the lemon juice immediately, and mix well, as it helps to keep the apples from browning. Add the flour, cinnamon, nutmeg, and allspice (if using) and mix well until the apples are evenly coated.

4. Preheat the oven to 375°F and grease a 10-inch pie pan. Remove the dough from the refrigerator and roll out each disk on a lightly floured piece of wax paper or parchment paper to approximately 1/4-inch thick. Transfer one rolled-out piece of dough to the pie pan and press it in gently, making sure there are no air pockets beneath the dough. The dough should come up and slightly spill over the sides of the pan.

5. Pour the apple mixture into the pie pan, pressing down gently to make sure it is level. Top the apples with the other piece of dough. Cut off any excess overhanging dough and pinch the corners of the crusts together.

6. Using a fork, gently pierce the upper crust evenly across the surface to create ventilation holes. Bake for 50 minutes, until the top crust is golden brown. Cool on a rack for 20 minutes before serving.

In 1989, the first Nuts 4 Nuts cart appeared in New York City, selling freshly made Buenos Aires–style honey-roasted nuts. Today, there are over one hundred of these carts throughout the City. You can always tell when there is one nearby by the sweet smell that fills the air around the cart.

NUTS FOR NUTS

Serves 4 to 6

3 tablespoons water
1/3 cup sugar
2 cups raw nuts (peanuts, cashews, almonds, or a combination of all three)
2 teaspoons vanilla extract

1. Preheat the oven to 400°F. Line an 18 x 12-inch baking sheet with parchment paper and then spray the parchment with nonstick cooking spray.

2. Add the water and sugar to a medium saucepan. Bring to a boil over medium heat. When the sugar has dissolved, add the nuts and vanilla. Stir occasionally to coat the nuts.

3. After about 2 minutes, stir fast. After 1 more minute, the water will evaporate and the sugar will crystallize on the nuts. When this happens, turn off the heat and keep stirring. The sugar will begin to caramelize on the nuts and turn brown.

4. Transfer the nuts to the prepared baking sheet and spread them out in a single layer. Bake the nuts until the sugar begins to melt, 5 to 7 minutes. Stir the nuts and bake until they begin to turn brown in places, about 2 minutes more. Remove the nuts from the oven, stir to distribute the caramel, and let them cool completely before serving. Store the nuts in a covered container for 3 days.

You'll feel like you are watching a game at Citi Field or Yankee Stadium with our caramel corn. While this is meant to be eaten right away, if you want to make it ahead of time to eat later, you can. You'll just need to bake it in a low-temperature oven to keep it from getting soggy.

CARAMEL CORN

Serves 6 to 8

5 cups plain popped popcorn
1/4 cup nondairy butter
1 tablespoon extra-virgin olive oil
1/2 cup brown sugar
1 tablespoon maple syrup
1/2 teaspoon baking soda
1/4 cup nondairy semisweet chocolate chips

1. Line an 18 x 12-inch baking sheet with parchment paper and set aside. Put the popcorn into a large mixing bowl and set aside.

2. In a large saucepan over low heat, combine the butter and olive oil. Once the butter has melted, add the brown sugar and maple syrup and bring to a low boil. Cook 3 to 5 minutes, without stirring, until it turns a rich caramel color. Remove the caramel from the heat and mix in the baking soda. Pour the caramel over the popcorn and mix thoroughly. Pour the coated popcorn onto the prepared baking sheet and spread evenly into a single layer.

3. If you are going to eat the caramel corn right away, put the chocolate in a microwave-safe bowl and heat in the microwave for 2 minutes, stopping to stir every 30 seconds, until it is completely melted and smooth. Drizzle the melted chocolate over the top of the caramel corn.

4. If you are preparing this ahead of time, preheat the oven to 250°F. Place the baking sheet in the oven for 45 minutes, stirring every 15 minutes. This dries out the popcorn so that it does not get soggy. While the popcorn is drying, put the chocolate in a microwave-safe bowl and heat in the microwave for 2 minutes, stopping to stir every 30 seconds, until it is completely melted and smooth. Remove the popcorn from the oven and drizzle it with the melted chocolate. Allow the caramel corn to cool completely, then transfer it to airtight containers or bags and store at room temperature.

Cheesecake is one of the most iconic New York City desserts. New York–style cheesecake is unique in that it relies on heavy cream and sour cream to make it thick and dense. Many New Yorkers who move away from the area often have relatives send them frozen cheesecakes so they can have a taste of home. Since 1929, cheesecakes from Junior's in Brooklyn have been a New York City staple. Sadly, they don't make a vegan one yet—but we do. Try it topped with some homemade Blueberry Sauce (page 26).

NEW YORK CHEESECAKE

Serves 8 to 10

1 1/2 cups graham cracker crumbs
4 tablespoons nondairy butter, melted
4 (8-ounce) containers nondairy cream cheese, softened
3 tablespoons unbleached all-purpose flour
2 teaspoons lemon juice
1 1/2 cups sugar
2 teaspoons vanilla extract
Pinch salt
1/2 cup nondairy sour cream
2 tablespoons Ener-G Egg Replacer

1. Preheat the oven to 350°F. Lightly spray the bottom and sides of a 9-inch springform pan with nonstick cooking spray and set aside.

2. Combine the graham cracker crumbs and butter in a large mixing bowl and mix well with a fork. Use your fingers to press the mixture firmly and evenly into the prepared springform pan until it is a solid, packed 1/4-inch layer of crust lining the bottom and slightly up the sides of the pan. Bake the crust for 10 minutes. Remove it from the oven and allow it to cool before filling.

3. Combine the cream cheese, flour, lemon juice, sugar, vanilla, and salt in a large mixing bowl. Mix well, either with a handheld electric mixer or stand mixer, on medium speed until fully combined and the sugar is dissolved, about 3 minutes. The batter should be completely smooth. Beat in the sour cream and egg replacer on low speed until well blended.

4. Pour the batter into the partially baked crust and bake for 15 minutes. Reduce the heat to 250°F and bake for 40 to 60 minutes, until the center is set but still a little jiggly. Turn off the heat and let the cheesecake rest for 30 minutes in the oven. Remove the cheesecake from the oven and let it cool in the pan on a wire rack for at least 30 minutes. When the cheesecake is cool, run a knife carefully around the side of the cheesecake, but do not remove or release the side of the pan. Put the cheesecake in the refrigerator, uncovered, for at least 4 hours (preferably overnight).

5. When ready to serve, carefully run a knife along the side of the cheesecake to loosen it and remove the side of the pan. Store leftovers in the refrigerator for up to 5 days.

Michael: *On one of our first dates, on July 3, 2004, Ethan and I went for a long walk across the Brooklyn Bridge to get ice cream at the Brooklyn Ice Cream Factory. I had heard about it on TV and was dying to try it. Despite the fact that it was 90 degrees with 80 percent humidity, we hiked across the bridge and had some great ice cream. When we went vegan, I was determined to have ice cream that rich and creamy again and came up with a recipe that easily rivals the one that day.*

CHOCOLATE CHIP ICE CREAM

Makes 2 pints

2 (15-ounce) cans full-fat coconut milk
1 cup sugar
1 1/2 teaspoons vanilla extract
1 cup nondairy semisweet chocolate chips

1. Combine the coconut milk, sugar, and vanilla in a blender or the bowl of a stand mixer. Blend the mixture on high for 1 to 2 minutes or until creamy and smooth. Or use a mixer with the whisk attachment and mix for 2 minutes until fully combined and smooth. Place the mixture in the refrigerator for 2 hours to chill.

2. Transfer the ice cream base to an ice cream maker and follow the instructions for the machine. During the last 5 minutes of the ice cream maker's cycle, add the chocolate chips.

3. When the time is up, the ice cream will have a soft-serve consistency. Spoon the ice cream into a container, cover it, and put it in the freezer for at least 1 hour to harden.

Variation: To make chocolate ice cream, before adding the sugar and vanilla to the coconut milk, put 3 tablespoons of cocoa powder in a small bowl, and add enough of the coconut milk, 1 tablespoon at a time, to dissolve the cocoa powder. Mix well to dissolve the cocoa. When the cocoa is fully dissolved, add the cocoa mixture to the remaining coconut milk and continue with the recipe.

Ice Cream Parlors

The first ice cream parlor in America was opened in 1774 by Philip Lenzi, a confectioner from London, who opened a shop in what would become Lower Manhattan. Almost 220 years later, in 1960, Reuben Mattus, a Polish immigrant who lived in the Bronx, at the opposite end of New York City from Mr. Lenzi's shop, invented Häagen-Dazs ice cream. In recent years, artisan ice cream shops have been popping up all over the City. Many of these establishments offer vegan ice creams, making the presence of vegan ice cream a new fixture in New York City life.

The bakery display case at Peacefood Café in Union Square is a dessert lover's dream come true. Filled with a wide variety of cookies, cakes, and pastries, you cannot help but order something sweet no matter how full you are from your meal. One of our favorite treats to order is the banana bread. Treat yourself to some at home for dessert, or turn it into French toast (page 27) for breakfast.

BANANA BREAD

Makes 1 loaf

1 1/2 cups unbleached all-purpose flour
1/4 teaspoon salt
1 teaspoon baking soda
1 teaspoon baking powder
3/4 cup sugar
1/2 cup canola oil or other neutral oil (or 1/4 cup oil and 1/4 cup unsweetened apple-sauce)
1 cup mashed banana (about 3 medium bananas)
1/4 cup water
1/2 cup nondairy semisweet chocolate chips

1. Preheat the oven to 350°F. Lightly grease a 9 x 5-inch bread pan and set aside.

2. In a large bowl, sift together the flour, salt, baking soda, and baking powder and set aside

3. In a large mixing bowl, combine the sugar, oil, and banana. Mix with a hand mixer or stand mixer on medium speed until evenly blended, about 1 minute.

4. Reduce the speed of the mixer and alternately add the flour mixture and the water to the banana mixture, mixing well after each addition. Continue until all of the flour and water are mixed in. Increase the speed to medium and mix until thoroughly combined, about 2 minutes. Add the chocolate chips and mix at medium speed for another minute. Pour the mixture evenly into the prepared bread pan. Bake for 40 minutes or until a toothpick inserted in the center comes out dry.

5. Cool the banana bread for 10 minutes on a wire rack in the pan. Remove it from the pan and allow it to cool completely before slicing.

Note: If you are using this for Banana Bread French Toast (page 27), cut the loaf into 8 equal slices and allow them to dry out for at least 1 hour, preferably overnight, before dipping into the batter.

Ethan: Without this cake, I could very likely not be alive. At least that's what my father has said for the over fifty years that my parents have been married. When they were first dating, my mother suffered a ruptured appendix. My father helped bring her to the hospital where she had an emergency appendectomy. After she was released, she went to her parents' house in Albany to recover. While recovering, she baked this cake and brought it back to New York City as a thank-you gift to my father. My father, a huge pastry and cake fanatic, says that he took one taste of this cake and knew he would marry my mother. Growing up, my mother made this cake all of the time and nobody ever complained. I veganized her recipe, and it tastes exactly the same.

CHOCOLATE CHIP SOUR CREAM COFFEE CAKE

Serves 10 to 12

2 tablespoons unsweetened cocoa powder
1 1/2 cups sugar, divided
12 ounces nondairy semisweet chocolate chips
2 cups unbleached all-purpose flour
1 teaspoon baking powder
1 teaspoon baking soda
6 tablespoons water
4 1/2 teaspoons Ener-G Egg Replacer
1/2 cup vegan shortening
1 teaspoon vanilla extract
1 cup nondairy sour cream

1. Preheat the oven to 350°F. Lightly grease a 10-inch tube pan and set aside.

2. In a small mixing bowl, combine the cocoa, 1/2 cup of the sugar, and the chocolate chips. Mix well to ensure that all of the chips are evenly coated. Set aside.

3. In a medium mixing bowl, combine the flour, baking powder, and baking soda and set aside.

4. In a small bowl, whisk together the water and egg replacer until foamy and fully incorporated. Pour the mixture into the bowl of a stand mixer. Add the shortening and remaining 1 cup sugar to the egg replacer mixture and beat for 3 to 4 minutes, or until smooth. Add the vanilla and sour cream and beat for 2 minutes.

5. Add half of the flour mixture to the egg replacer mixture and beat on low speed until thoroughly incorporated. Add the remaining flour mixture and beat on medium-high speed for 2 more minutes, occasionally stopping to scrape down the side of the bowl.

6. Carefully add half of the batter to the prepared tube pan. Using a spatula, gently spread the batter into an even and level layer. Sprinkle half of the chocolate chip mixture evenly all over the surface of the batter in the pan. Make sure you are using both chocolate chips as well as

the sugar in the mixture. Carefully spread the remaining batter on top of the chocolate chips into an even, level layer. Top with the remaining chocolate chip mixture.

7. Bake the cake for 45 minutes. Insert a toothpick into the cake—if it comes out clean, the cake is done. Cool the cake for 15 minutes on a cooling rack before gently separating it from the tube pan.

Michael: *As a child with a mother from Brooklyn, I grew up hearing all about egg creams. To me, they sounded vile. Who in their right mind would want to drink raw eggs? It wasn't until well into my adulthood that I learned that an egg cream does not in fact contain eggs. It is simply milk, chocolate syrup, and seltzer. I have no clue why is it called an egg cream. In honor of my mother's roots, I came up with a vegan version of her childhood favorite. There are no measurements for this recipe, it is all done right in the glass, so the size of the glass is very important. (See photo on the cover.)*

BROOKLYN EGG CREAM

Serves 1

Chocolate Syrup (page 167) or store-bought nondairy chocolate syrup
Chock Full o' Nuts Milk (page 7) or store-bought nondairy milk
Seltzer, to fill the glass

1. Pour 3/4 inch of chocolate syrup into the bottom of a 12-ounce glass. (If you have an old-fashioned milkshake glass, even better.) Top the syrup with 1 inch of milk. Add a long spoon to the glass.

2. Fill the glass halfway with seltzer. Stir only at the bottom of the glass to mix the chocolate with the milk. Fill the glass with more seltzer until the foam reaches the top of the glass, being careful that the foam doesn't spill over the side. The end product should be a sweet chocolate soda with about 1 inch of foam on top. Add a straw and serve immediately!

CHOCOLATE SYRUP

Makes 1 1/2 cups

In the early 1900s, H. Fox & Co. opened in Brooklyn and began selling Fox's U-Bet Chocolate Sauce. This sauce quickly became the chocolate sauce of New York City. We've re-created their rich, delicious, chocolatey sauce, and it is perfect for using in an egg cream (page 166) or as a topping for Chocolate Chip Ice Cream (page 162).

    3/4 cup cocoa powder
    1 cup sugar
    Pinch salt
    1 cup boiling water, divided
    1 1/2 teaspoons vanilla extract

1. In a small saucepan, whisk together the cocoa, sugar, and salt. Add 1/2 cup of the boiling water and stir well until all the cocoa is incorporated and the mixture is completely smooth. Let this sit for 4 minutes.

2. Add the remaining 1/2 cup boiling water and whisk to incorporate. Bring the sauce to a simmer over medium heat. Simmer for 2 minutes, stirring occasionally with a silicone spatula, making sure to scrape the bottom of the pan to prevent any cocoa from sticking and burning. Remove the saucepan from the heat and stir in the vanilla.

3. Let the chocolate syrup cool, then transfer it to a container with a tight-fitting lid and refrigerate until needed. This will keep in the refrigerator for 3 weeks.

Walk down Mulberry Street in Little Italy on a hot summer day and you'll find vendors scooping various flavors of Italian ices from their pushcarts into small paper cups. This refreshing treat of fresh summer fruit and ice is just the thing to cool you down.

ITALIAN ICES

Serves 8

3 cups fresh fruit (such as strawberries, blueberries, pineapple, or watermelon)
2 to 4 tablespoons granulated sugar (depending on the level of sweetness you want)
1 tablespoon fresh lemon juice
3 cups ice, divided

1. Combine the fruit, sugar, lemon juice, and 2 cups of the ice in a food processor or high-speed blender. Process until the mixture is chunky, then add the remaining 1 cup ice. Process until completely smooth.

2. Pour the mixture into ice cube trays and place them in the freezer for 2 hours. After 2 hours, place the frozen cubes into a food processor and pulse to break the cubes into slush.

3. Scoop the Italian ices into bowls or small paper cups for a more authentic experience. Store Italian ices, covered, in the freezer for up to 2 weeks.

"Whoever is born in New York is ill-equipped to deal with any other city: all other cities seem, at best, a mistake, and, at worst, a fraud. No other city is so spitefully incoherent."

— James Baldwin

Ethan: *Literally translated from Yiddish as "almond bread," mandelbrodt is like a biscotti but softer due to the higher oil content. This Eastern European Jewish cookie was a favorite with Jewish immigrants to the Lower East Side. My grandmother has made these since she was a little girl, and I grew up eating her version of them. Fast-forward to when I met Michael's cousin Karen. She makes hers with a dusting of a mixture of sugar, cocoa powder, and cinnamon before baking. This was so mind-blowingly awesome to me that I decided to hybridize these two recipes when creating this vegan blended-family version. Enjoy them like we do, with a freshly brewed cup of coffee—and be sure to dunk them in your coffee!*

MANDELBRODT

Makes 12 cookies

2 cups unbleached all-purpose flour
2 teaspoons baking powder
2 tablespoons ground flax seed
6 tablespoons warm water
1/2 cup canola oil or other neutral oil
3/4 cup sugar, divided
2 teaspoons vanilla extract
1/4 teaspoon almond extract
1/2 cup nondairy semisweet chocolate chips
1 tablespoon cocoa powder
1 teaspoon ground cinnamon

1. Preheat the oven to 350°F. Line an 18 x 12-inch baking sheet with parchment paper and set aside. In a medium mixing bowl, sift the together the flour and baking powder and set aside.

2. In the bowl of an electric stand mixer, add the flax seed and water and whisk on high speed for 3 to 4 minutes, until the mixture is slightly frothy and has a sticky, egg-like consistency to it. Change to the paddle attachment, add the oil and 1/2 cup of the sugar. Mix on high speed for 1 minute, until the mixture has an even consistency. Add the vanilla and almond extracts and mix for 1 minute more.

3. Add half of the flour mixture to the flax mixture and mix on medium-low speed. Once the flour is fully incorporated, add the remaining flour mixture and mix on medium speed until a cookie-like dough forms. Add the chocolate chips and mix for 1 minute more.

4. Use a spatula to scrape down the side of the bowl and roll the dough into a ball. Wet your hands periodically with cold water as this helps to keep the dough from sticking. Hand shape the dough into a log that is approximately 2 inches shorter than the length of the baking sheet and arrange the log on the prepared baking sheet. Wet your hands and gently press down to flatten to approximately 1/3-inch thick and shape into a long rectangle.

5. In a small bowl, combine the remaining 1/4 cup sugar, cocoa, and cinnamon. Pour the mixture slowly into a strainer or sifter and lightly dust a thin, even coating over the top of the dough. Bake the dough for 15 minutes. Remove it from the oven and quickly slice it into 1-inch sections. After making each slice, use a fork to flip each piece onto its side, cut-side up. Bake again for an additional 10 minutes. Watch the oven closely to make sure they don't start to burn. Remove the baking sheet from the oven and cool the cookies for at least 10 minutes before serving.

As we were finishing writing this book, the annual Giglio Feast was occurring two blocks from our apartment in Williamsburg. This Italian festival has been an annual event since 1903. During the festival, several blocks in the area are closed to cars and are filled with carnival games, rides, and, of course, Italian food. The only vegan food option at the feast is zeppole from Dee Best. Zeppole are a staple of Italian street festivals all over New York City. These fried balls of dough are tossed with powdered sugar and make braving the huge festival crowds worthwhile. We realized we couldn't have a New York City-themed cookbook and not include a recipe for zeppole.

ZEPPOLE

Makes 24

1 pound Pizza Dough (page 8) or store-bought vegan pizza dough
Canola oil or other neutral oil, for deep-frying
Extra-virgin olive oil, for deep-frying
Confectioners' sugar

1. Cut the pizza dough into quarters. Roll each quarter into a rope about 3/4-inch thick. Cut each rope into 2 1/2-inch pieces and form each piece into a ring. Alternatively, roll out the dough on a lightly floured work surface to 1/2-inch thickness. Pull off pieces of dough and roll into golf ball–size pieces. Poke your finger through each ball of dough, but don't open it to a full doughnut shape. This hole will help the zeppole fry more evenly.

2. Pour 1 inch of canola oil and 1 inch olive oil into a large frying pan. Heat the oil over medium heat until a deep-fry thermometer registers 375°F. Working in batches, fry the zeppole until they are nicely golden brown, about 2 minutes per side. Using a slotted spoon, transfer the zeppole to paper towels to drain. Let them cool slightly.

3. Sift the confectioners' sugar over the zeppole or, if you really want to be authentic, put the zeppole in a paper bag, add the confectioners' sugar, and shake gently to coat them. These are meant to be eaten almost immediately. If you are not going to eat them right away, hold off on adding the powdered sugar until you are ready to eat.

Ten
BEING VEGAN IN
NEW YORK CITY

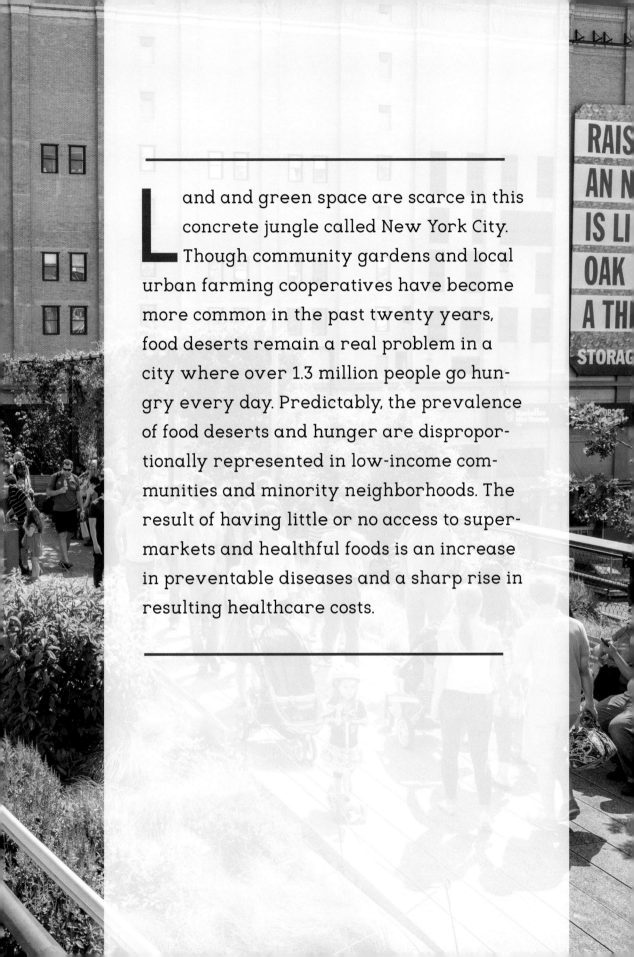

L and and green space are scarce in this concrete jungle called New York City. Though community gardens and local urban farming cooperatives have become more common in the past twenty years, food deserts remain a real problem in a city where over 1.3 million people go hungry every day. Predictably, the prevalence of food deserts and hunger are disproportionally represented in low-income communities and minority neighborhoods. The result of having little or no access to supermarkets and healthful foods is an increase in preventable diseases and a sharp rise in resulting healthcare costs.

Why Being Vegan Matters to NYC

(photos by the authors taken at Woodstock Farm Sanctuary)

One in three adult New Yorkers is overweight and over one in five is obese. Even more disturbing, one in five kindergarten students and one in four Head Start children in New York City is obese. Forty percent of elementary school kids in New York City are overweight, which puts them at a significantly increased risk of developing type 2 diabetes. Over seven hundred thousand New Yorkers have type 2 diabetes and nearly one-third of them are unaware that they have it. One in four New Yorkers has high blood pressure and one in three adults lives with cardiovascular disease. Heart disease and stroke are the leading causes of death here. The highest rates of obesity are found in neighborhoods with no supermarkets, where smaller groceries, convenience stores, or bodegas provide a selection of high-calorie, mostly packaged foods with few fruits and vegetables.

Heart disease, stroke, type 2 diabetes, and obesity have conclusively been linked to diets high in animal-derived fats and cholesterol. Conversely, numerous evidence-based, peer-reviewed scientific studies indicate that a whole-food, plant-based diet has been shown to reverse heart disease, type 2 diabetes, and obesity. Sadly, and unbeknown to many, the federal government is playing a key role in the preservation of food deserts and the promotion of these preventable diseases in low-income and minority populations by subsidizing certain aspects of the food industry. David Robinson Simon points out in *Meatonomics* that the actual cost of a McDonald's Big Mac is $13: consumers pay $5 for the burger while the rest of us pay $8 in "hidden costs" that can be measured in increased healthcare costs and environmental damage resulting from the production and consumption of this disease-causing food. The federal government also directly subsidizes the meat and dairy industries to the tune of about $38 billion annually, keeping the costs of unhealthy animal-derived food products artificially low.

Shockingly, annual federal subsidies for fruits and vegetables are a paltry 0.04 percent of that number, at just $17 million. People eat what they can afford, and the government makes sure that low-income families can afford the very foods that are making them disproportionally sick with heart disease, high cholesterol, type 2 diabetes, and obesity. A more sensible plan to reduce these healthcare costs, as well as promote health and wellness among the most vulnerable in our society, would be to start heavily subsidizing health-promoting fruits and vegetables, resulting in a huge economic stimulus.

The environmental costs of animal agriculture disproportionally affect coastal cities, like New York, that are particularly susceptible to the effects of climate change. It is well established that a one-degree Celsius rise in global mean temperature has resulted in a six-meter sea level rise. Carbon dioxide (CO_2) levels are a significant driver in rising global temperatures. Though the transportation sector is well known to be a large contributor to rising CO_2 levels, producing livestock and their by-products far exceeds the transportation sector. Animal agriculture pushes thirty-two thousand million tons of CO_2 into the atmosphere annually, accounting for over half of all worldwide greenhouse gas emissions. Methane is an even more powerful greenhouse gas than CO_2. Methane can trap up to one hundred times the heat in the atmosphere that CO_2 can in a five-year period and seventy-two times more than CO_2 in a twenty-year period. Methane also dissipates from the atmosphere within a decade, far more quickly than CO_2, which can take upward of a hundred years. Thus, a reduction in methane production would yield a quicker reduction in greenhouse gasses.

So where does methane come from? While some of it comes from the production of coal and natural gas, the overwhelming majority is produced by waste decomposition in landfills, from manure management from livestock, and from ruminant digestion, or "cow farts." Cows alone produce 150 billion gallons of methane per day. Even more damaging than methane or CO_2 is nitrous oxide, a greenhouse gas with nearly three hundred times the climate-changing potential of CO_2, and that stays in the atmosphere for 150 years. The livestock sector alone is responsible for 65 percent of all human-related emissions of nitrous oxide. All of these facts point to one very obvious solution to reducing greenhouse gas emissions: stop raising and killing animals for food. As the United Nations Climate Summit in 2014 pointed out, reducing methane emissions "can have immediate impact and slow the increase in global temperatures expected over the next 35 years by as much as 0.6°C while benefiting people's health and the production of food." If our culture shifted from eating an animal-based diet to a plant-based, vegan diet, we could quite literally exert immediate effects that will reverse climate change. As an American coastal city with so much to lose, New York City should lead the way in going vegan. Adopting a sustainable plant-based, vegan diet will reverse climate change, promote health, and address issues of food scarcity.

Why We Choose to Live Vegan

For us, there is still a more compelling call to veganism than all of the aforementioned reasons. Going vegan is in the best interests of all animals, both human and nonhuman. As vegans and animal rights activists, we are often accused of caring more about animals than people. In truth, we care deeply about humans and nonhumans alike. Adopting a vegan diet can significantly address human hunger, as we could feed eight hundred million people with the grain fed to livestock animals. Some of the most vulnerable people in our society are charged with the gruesome and dangerous work of turning animals into food. Over half a million people in the United States work in slaughterhouses and processing facilities. This workforce is predominantly composed of lower-income individuals and nearly 40 percent of these individuals were born outside the United States, many of whom are undocumented workers. With limited options for employment, they accept these hard, dangerous, and low-paying jobs. Due to their tenuous and vulnerable legal status, they routinely avoid reporting safety concerns, injuries, or other issues for fear of losing their jobs,

being reported, and being deported. The psychological effects of this work on slaughterhouse workers are well documented. Many suffer from PTSD as they become desensitized to the suffering of others. They experience higher than normal rates of domestic violence, anxiety, and substance abuse. Adopting a vegan diet is in no small part a rejection of this extreme exploitation of the most vulnerable people in our communities.

Yet the most vulnerable individuals on Earth lack the capacity to advocate for themselves. Though nonhuman animals are different than we, they share some of the traits that we most value: the capacity to feel joy, love, pain, and suffering. Anyone who has lived with cats or dogs knows just how unique and complex they are. We love our companion animals and many of us consider them members of our families. Even so, we draw arbitrary distinctions when it comes to farmed animals. We make absurd claims about their relative intelligence and sentience in order to justify their exploitation. Pigs are far more intelligent than dogs, having repeatedly been shown to have the intellectual capabilities of a three-year-old human child, but we nevertheless brutally slaughter and consume over 110 million of these individuals each year in the United States. However, when we hear about the different arbitrary distinctions drawn between animals in other cultures, we often become outraged. In the United States and Europe, the outcry against the annual Yulin Lychee and Dog Meat Festival in China is deafening. Having determined that dogs deserve our compassion, love, and mercy, we are understandably appalled when other cultures do not share our values and kill dogs for food without regard to their individuality or their capacity to suffer. The pigs and dogs raised for food both suffer, so why do we have such a different reaction to one versus the other?

The justification for this hypocrisy is speciesism: discrimination that assigns different values, rights, and considerations to individuals solely based on their species membership. This

discrimination doesn't happen by accident. Speciesism is programmed into all of us at an early, often preconscious age. Normally, children show an innate curiosity and kinship with animals. We socialize children with animals, putting friendly images of animals on their clothing and bedding and using animals as an educational tool in books. When a child lacks empathy or demonstrates aggressive and abusive behavior toward animals, we become concerned, as studies show that many of these children grow up to become sociopaths. Regardless of how much a child may love animals, at some point we teach them which animals we choose to love and which we choose to eat. We impart this as being just a matter of fact—that it's just the way life is. We will ridicule a child who rebels against this distinction and call him or her sentimental or childish, implying that the adult thing to do is to detach from our innate sense of compassion and empathy. In so doing, we betray not only the animals, but our children as well.

Though it could have been argued in the past that eating animals was a necessary evil, that argument is neither valid nor reasonable today. Since we can no longer claim a nutritional requirement to eat animals, or their products and secretions, we cite our habits, traditions, cultural influences, convenience, or pleasure as the justification. But these are just excuses, and not valid moral justifications for the exploitation, harm, and suffering we impose on these sentient beings. As Jeremy Bentham, the eighteenth-century English philosopher famously said in regard to animals, "The question is not, 'Can they reason?' nor, 'Can they talk?' but, 'Can they suffer?'" Why should the law refuse its protection to any sensitive being?

Surely it is no coincidence that the best thing for human health, the health of our planet, and for the animals with whom we share this Earth is the very same thing. Adopting a plant-based diet and choosing to live vegan is the inevitable next step in our evolution toward becoming a more sustainable and just society. Lucky for us, it can be a delicious and fulfilling next step that is easily adapted to our traditions and cultural influences, as we hope this book has demonstrated.

"London is satisfied, Paris is resigned, but New York is always hopeful. Always it believes that something good is about to come off, and it must hurry to meet it."
— Dorothy Parker

The Vegan Restaurants of New York City

We New Yorkers enjoy an embarrassment of riches when it comes to availability and variety of all-vegan restaurants. It isn't an exaggeration to say that there seems to be a new one opening nearly every month. While Staten Island is still the only borough without an all-vegan restaurant, there are still many vegan-friendly vegetarian options there. However, in this section, we want to single out the brave and trailblazing restaurateurs who are paving the way forward, into the twenty-first century. We know that the bourgeoning expansion of successful all-vegan restaurants in New York and around the world will continue as more and more people wake up each day to the desire to eat more sustainably, healthfully, and ethically. To all of these courageous NYC vegan restaurants, we thank you for your leadership and for feeding New York such delicious vegan food. You are truly changing the world, one meal at a time.

BRONX

Jolo's Kitchen
Vegan's Delight

BROOKLYN

24 Scoops and Plates
Bunna Cafe
Champs Diner
Dun-Well Doughnuts
Four Seasons Bakery and Juice Bar
Greenforce Juice
Hartwell Vegetarian
Loving Hut
Mint Vegan
Modern Love
Riverdel
Shangri-La Vegetarian
Sun in Bloom
Toad Style
VSPOT
Wild Ginger

MANHATTAN

Angelica Kitchen
Avant Garden

Beyond Sushi
Blossom (multiple locations)
Blossom du Jour (multiple locations)
by CHLOE (multiple locations)
Café 5C
Candle 79
Candle Cafe
Candle Cafe West
Caravan of Dreams
Cinnamon Snail
Delice & Sarrasin
Double Zero
Erin McKenna's Bakery
Franchia
Gingersnap's Organic
HanGawi
Harmony Kitchen
Jivamuktea Café
Kajitsu
Ladybird
Lantern
Mother of Pearl
peacefood cafe (multiple locations)
Sacred Chow
Seasoned Vegan
Terri (multiple locations)
The Green Roll
Urban Vegan Cafe
VSPOT
V Burger
Vegan Divas
Vita Vegan Paradise
VLife

QUEENS

Jujube Tree
Veggie Castle II

Acknowledgements

Writing this cookbook has been a labor of love, made all the easier with the support and encouragement of our many friends and family. We could easily write another chapter just expressing our gratitude to each and every one of you for the inspiration we've drawn from your positivity and encouragement. We know how fortunate we are to have so many loving friends and family who have believed in us and rooted for us since we started our blog and undertook writing this book. There are a few individuals who we need to single out in our gratitude for their uniquely significant contributions that helped this book you are holding come into existence.

First and foremost, a heartfelt thank you to our "vegan fairy godmother," JL Fields. You encouraged us to start a blog on a rainy train ride into New York City in May 2013, and four months later Vegan Mos was born. You have not stopped encouraging and supporting us along our journey. Thank you for your love and friendship.

Thank you to our publisher, Jon Robertson, and the incredible team at Vegan Heritage Press. You took a chance on us and we will forever be grateful to you for this opportunity.

Jackie Sobon, you're a rock star. You took our food and effortlessly turned it into works of art. You have been so fun to work with and your insights and guidance have been invaluable.

Alan Cumming, we have been longtime fans of both your stage and screen work, but it is your tireless activism for LGBTQ and animal rights that makes you a star to us. We are humbled by your generosity in agreeing to write the foreword to our book—thank you!

Our recipe testers: Brandie Bloggins; Christine Day; Robin Fetter; Jennifer Lewis; Dorothy Miller; and "The Food Duo," Carmella Lanni and Carlo Giardina. Thank you all for your time, energy, and invaluable feedback.

To the many vegan food bloggers and cookbook authors who guided us along the way when we first became vegan, thank you for sharing your knowledge. You continue to inspire us.

To our friends Jasmin Singer and Mariann Sullivan, thank you for your friendship and for believing in Vegan Mos. The opportunities you have given us through Our Hen House have allowed us to share our work with more people than we would have ever been able to otherwise. Thank you for giving us a platform to help do our part to change the world for animals.

Michael: To my mother, Judy Suchman, thank you for teaching me how to cook and sharing your recipes with me. I've come a long way since pancakes and boxed baking mixes. To my father, Jerry Suchman, thank for teaching me the invaluable lesson that even on an electric stove, food can catch fire.

Ethan: To my father, Mel Ciment, thank you for being so progressive back in the 1970s by encouraging both of your sons to learn how to cook. To my mother, Barbara Ciment, I thank you for allowing me to cook and bake with you since I was a little boy. Mom, some of my most cherished early memories are of time spent with you in the kitchen. Along with my beloved grandmothers, Ethel Kagan and Regina Ciment, you taught me that food not only nourishes our bodies but also feeds our souls with the love and traditions we infuse into it. Thank you for imparting this most valuable gift to me.

Finally, to Riley and Charlie, who missed out on belly rubs and kisses while we were busy in the kitchen cooking or on the computer writing this book. We love you and always appreciate your patience with us. Thanks for being such enthusiastic tasters.

About the Authors

Michael Suchman and Ethan Ciment founded and run the popular blog VeganMos.com. Together, they were named one of the top ten male vegan bloggers for 2015 by *VegNews* magazine and won a 2016 Bloggy Award as one of the top vegan blogs to follow from the same magazine. The Vegan Mos regularly speak and hold food demos at veg fests around the country and are often featured guests on the Our Hen House podcast, which reaches over thirty thousand listeners worldwide.

Michael Suchman

Michael has been hooked on cooking since the age of seven and believes he becomes his true self when he's in the kitchen. Michael believes passionately in vegan food as activism. He is a certified vegan life coach and educator through the Main Street Vegan Academy. He is also a certified Food for Life instructor through the Physicians Committee for Responsible Medicine. Michael is a recovering lawyer, having practiced in the field of corporate litigation for twelve years. He is also an accomplished photographer whose work can be seen in private collections in New York, Palm Beach, and Los Angeles.

photo by Derek Goodwin

Ethan J. Ciment

photo by Susan Shek

Ethan is a podiatric surgeon in private practice in New York City. He is a fellow of The American College of Foot and Ankle Orthopedics and Medicine. Ethan is the founder and director of The Chelsea Foot and Ankle Center in Manhattan, where he treats the entire spectrum of foot and ankle medicine and surgery. Raised in an Orthodox Jewish family and coming from a long line of kosher butchers, Ethan woke up in his late thirties to the realities of animal exploitation when caring for his ailing dog, Chandler. Having discovered the health benefits of a plant-based diet, Ethan decided to go fully vegan. He now actively promotes the health benefits of a plant-based, vegan diet to his patients. Ethan serves on the board of directors of Woodstock Farm Sanctuary, an organization that is near and dear to his heart.

Ethan and Michael live in Brooklyn with their two neurotic but lovable vegan dogs, Riley and Charlie.

Index

"My favorite thing about New York is the people, because I think they're misunderstood. I don't think people realize how kind New York people are."

— Bill Murray

Ast...
Ditmars Blvd N·Q

Astoria Blvd.
M60 LGA Airport N·Q ✈

SECOND AV
FIRST AV

St
31 ST
36 ST
STEINWAY ST

96 ST

21 ST
30 Av N·Q
Steinway St M·R
30 AV

N

Grand Central Terminal ♿
Metro-North Railroad
Subway S 4 5 6 7 except S
Bus - M1 M2 M3 M4
M42 M101 M102 M103 Q32
NY Airport Service ✈
Newark Airport Express ✈

Q

R M

Broadway N·Q

6 St

86 ST

86 St
4·5·6

UPPER
EAST
SIDE

LONG
ISLAND
CITY

36 Av N·Q
36 St M·R

79 ST

VERNON BLVD

39 Av N·Q

77 St
6

72 ST

21 St
Queens-
bridge

39 Av N·Q

YORK AV

Roosevelt
Island F

LEXINGTON AV

68 St
Hunter College
6

65 ST
63 ST

ROOSEVELT
ISL

51 AV

Queensboro
Plaza N·Q·7

exington
/63 St

Lexington Av/59 St
N·Q·R

Court Sq-23 St E·M

Court Sq 7

59 St
4·5·6
Lexington Av/53 St E·M·6

R

21 St

5 Av
59 St
N·Q·R

51 St
6

5 Av/53 St E·M

50 Sts
Rockefeller Ctr

Metric Conversions and Equivalents

The recipes in this book have not been tested with metric measurements, so some variations may occur.

LIQUID	
US	**METRIC**
1 tsp	5 ml
1 tbs	15 ml
2 tbs	30 ml
1/4 cup	60 ml
1/3 cup	75 ml
1/2 cup	120 ml
2/3 cup	150 ml
3/4 cup	180 ml
1 cup	240 ml
1 1/4 cups	300 ml
1 1/3 cups	325 ml
1 1/2 cups	350 ml
1 2/3 cups	375 ml
1 3/4 cups	400 ml
2 cups (1 pint)	475 ml
3 cups	720 ml
4 cups (1 quart)	945 ml

GENERAL METRIC CONVERSION FORMULAS	
Ounces to grams	ounces x 28.35 = grams
Grams to ounces	grams x 0.035 = ounces
Pounds to grams	pounds x 435.5 = grams
Pounds to kilograms	pounds x 0.45 = kilograms
Cups to liters	cups x 0.24 = liters
Fahrenheit to Celsius	(°F - 32) x 5 ÷ 9 = °C
Celsius to Fahrenheit	(°C x 9) ÷ 5 + 32 = °F

WEIGHT	
US	**METRIC**
1/2 oz	14 g
1 oz	28 g
1 1/2 oz	43 g
2 oz	57 g
2 1/2 oz	71 g
4 oz	113 g
5 oz	142 g
6 oz	170 g
7 oz	200 g
8 oz (1/2 lb)	227 g
9 oz	255 g
10 oz	284 g
11 oz	312 g
12 oz	340 g
13 oz	368 g
14 oz	400 g
15 oz	425 g
16 oz (1 lb)	454 g

OVEN TEMPERATURE		
°F	**Gas Mark**	**°C**
250	1/2	120
275	1	140
300	2	150
325	3	165
350	4	180
375	5	190
400	6	200
425	7	220
450	8	230
475	9	240
500	10	260
550	Broil	290

LENGTH	
US	**METRIC**
1/2 inch	1.25 cm
1 inch	2.5 cm
6 inches	15 cm
8 inches	20 cm
10 inches	25 cm
12 inches	30 cm